P9-DDI-596

Birds of Virginia

Field Guide

WITHDRAWN

by Stan Tekiela

ADVENTURE PUBLICATIONS, INC.
CAMBRIDGE, MINNESOTA

TO MY WIFE KATHERINE AND DAUGHTER ABIGAIL
WITH ALL MY LOVE

ACKNOWLEDGMENTS:

Special thanks to Anthony Hertzel for range maps, and Dr. Charles R. Blem, Department of Biology, Virginia Commonwealth University, for reviewing them. Special thanks also to Sandy Livoti for her exceptional eye to detail.

Book design and illustrations by Jonathan Norberg

Photo credits by photographer and page number:

Cover photo: Northern Cardinal by Maslowski Wildlife Productions
Brian Collins: 2, 202, 276 **Cornell Laboratory of Ornithology**: 82, 84 (female), 90 (perching), 252 (both) **Dudley Edmondson**: 12, 20, 24 (soaring), 62 (soaring), 64 (breeding), 66 (all), 86 (non-breeding adult, white juvenile), 92, 94, 104, 108 (both), 114, 126, 128, 142 (in flight), 148, 154 (both), 156 (male), 162, 174 (soaring), 190 (both), 200, 206 (all), 220 (male), 230 (breeding), 238, 250 (male), 258 (perching, soaring), 260, 262 (winter, displaying), 266, 296 (in flight), 300 (breeding), 308 (breeding), 310 (adult), 318 (male, winter male), 320, 322 (male), 330 **Carrol Henderson**: 102 **Kevin T. Karlson**: 22 (soaring), 44, 46, 48, 54 (both), 134, 146 (female), 158, 232, 254, 256, 298 (winter), 302 (breeding), 306, 326 **Bruce Leventhal**: 314 **Bill Marchel**. 4, 30 (male), 32, 38, 84 (male), 98, 116 (white-striped), 122, 152, 170, 174 (perching), 188, 218, 220 (female), 270, 272 (both), 282, 288, 312, 316 (in flight) **Maslowski Wildlife Productions**: 28, 78, 100, 124, 130, 138, 144, 208, 216, 236, 292, 324, 334 **Arthur Morris**: 56, 146 (male) **Steve Mortensen**: 8, 30 (female), 34 (male), 36 (both), 58 (both), 62 (perching), 72, 74, 76 (both), 110, 180, 192, 226, 234, 274, 318 (female) **Warren Nelson**: 34 (female), 90 (female), 156 (female), 322 (female) **John Pennoyer**: 96, 140, 280, 286 (male) **Brian E. Small**: 18, 22 (perching), 50, 64 (winter), 68, 120, 132 (winter), 136, 166, 168 (breeding), 172, 178, 198, 212, 222, 230 (winter), 240, 242, 246, 284, 286 (yellow male), 290, 298 (breeding), 300 (winter, juvenile), 302 (in flight), 308 (winter), 332 **Stan Tekiela**: 6 (both), 10, 14, 16, 26 (both), 40 (both), 42 (breeding), 52, 60, 70, 80 (both), 86 (breeding, molting juvenile), 88, 106, 112, 116 (tan-striped), 118, 132 (breeding), 142 (perching), 150, 160, 164, 182, 184, 186, 194, 204, 210, 214, 224, 228, 244, 248 (gray morph), 250 (female), 258 (juvenile), 268, 278, 294 (in flight), 296 (perching), 302 (winter), 304, 310 (juvenile), 316 (swimming), 336 **Brian K. Wheeler**: 24 (perching), 176 (both), 264 (all) **Jim Zipp**: 42 (winter), 196, 248 (red morph), 294 (perching), 328

To the best of the publisher's knowledge, all photos except the female Indigo Bunting were of live birds.

TABLE OF CONTENTS
Introduction

Sample Page

The Birds

WHY WATCH BIRDS IN VIRGINIA?

Millions of people have discovered bird feeding. It's a simple and enjoyable way to bring the beauty of birds closer to your home. Watching birds at your feeder often leads to a lifetime pursuit of bird identification. The *Birds of Virginia Field Guide* is for those who want to identify common birds of Virginia.

There are over 800 species of birds found in North America. In Virginia alone there have been more than 425 different kinds of birds recorded throughout the years. These bird sightings were diligently recorded by hundreds of bird watchers and became part of the official state record. From these valuable records, I've chosen 140 of the most common birds of Virginia to include in this field guide.

Bird watching, often called birding, is the largest spectator sport in America. Its outstanding popularity in Virginia is due, in part, to an unusually rich and abundant birdlife. Why are there so many birds? One reason is open space. Virginia is over 42,000 square miles (109,200 sq. km), making it the thirty-fifth largest state. Despite its large size, only about 6.8 million people call Virginia home. On average, that is only 174 people per square mile (67 per sq. km). Most of these people are located in and around only three major cities.

Open space is not the only reason there is such an abundance of birds. It's also the diversity of habitat. On a broad scope, the state can be divided into three main regions—the Atlantic Coastal Plain, Piedmont Plateau and Appalachian Mountains.

The Atlantic Coastal Plain is a broad lowland region that extends along most of the U.S. eastern seaboard. In Virginia this region is exemplified by the Chesapeake Bay. Separating the mainland from the East Shore, it is one of the largest estuaries in North America. Estuaries are rich habitats where fresh water flowing out of the land from rivers mixes with saltwater from the ocean. This habitat supports an extremely diverse bird population that includes pelicans and Ospreys, and many species of shorebirds.

The Atlantic Coastal Plain in Virginia has 112 miles (180 km) of coastline, which is home to many ocean-loving birds such as the colony-nesting Royal Tern and surf-running Sanderling. It also has many freshwater and saltwater marshes. These marshes are great places to see water birds such as Tricolored Herons.

Inland from the coastal plain is a region known as the Piedmont Plateau. The foothills and rolling topography here are a mix of cultivated fields, pastures, abandoned fields and woodlands. This region offers habitat for waterfowl in lakes and rivers. Sparrows are found in abandoned fields. Forest birds, such as warblers, live in pine and oak woods. The Piedmont is a great place to see an altogether different group of birds than those found in the Atlantic Coastal Plain.

The Appalachian Mountains in western Virginia add to the great diversity of bird species in the state. This mountainous habitat is entirely different from habitats seen elsewhere in Virginia. Birds that are more characteristic of the northern forest, such as the Red-breasted Nuthatch and Dark-eyed Junco, are found here.

Virginia's rivers, lakes and reservoirs play a large part in its bird populations. These places compose a substantial aquatic habitat for species such as Belted Kingfishers and Great Blue Herons.

The geographic location of Virginia also makes it a great place to see birds. Positioned in the middle of a major migratory route that is used by a wide variety of species, Virginia is one of the best states to see millions of migrating birds in spring and fall.

Finally, varying weather in Virginia attracts many different birds. The higher elevations in western Virginia are much colder and snowier than habitats near the ocean. Winter temperatures in the mountains may stay below freezing for weeks and winds can be fierce. Summers there are cooler and drier than on the coast.

Whether watching a nesting colony of herons and egrets near the Chesapeake Bay or welcoming back wintering shorebirds, bird watchers enjoy variety and excitement in the birds of Virginia as each season turns to the next.

OBSERVE WITH A STRATEGY;
TIPS FOR IDENTIFYING BIRDS

Identifying birds isn't as difficult as you might think. By simply following a few basic strategies, you can increase your chances of successfully identifying most birds you see! One of the first and easiest things to do when you see a new bird is to note its color. (Also, since this book is organized by color, you will go right to that color section to find it.)

Next, note the size of the bird. A strategy to quickly estimate size is to select a small-, medium- and large-sized bird to use for reference. For example, most people are familiar with robins. A robin, measured from tip of the bill to tip of the tail, is 10 inches (25 cm) long. Using the robin as an example of a medium-sized bird, select two other birds, one smaller and one larger. Many people use a House Sparrow, at about 6 inches (15 cm), and an American Crow, about 18 inches (45 cm). When you see a bird that you don't know, you can quickly ask yourself, "Is it smaller than a robin, but larger than a sparrow?" When you look in your field guide to help identify your bird, you'll know it's roughly between 6 and 10 inches (15 to 25 cm) long. This will help to narrow your choices.

Next, note the size, shape and color of the bill. Is it long, short, thick, thin, pointed, blunt, curved or straight? Seed-eating birds, such as Northern Cardinals, have bills that are thick and strong enough to crack even the toughest seeds. Birds that sip nectar, such as Ruby-throated Hummingbirds, need long thin bills to reach deep into flowers. Hawks and owls tear their prey with very sharp, curving bills. Sometimes, just noting the bill shape can help you decide if the bird is a woodpecker, finch, grosbeak, blackbird or bird of prey.

Next, take a look around and note the habitat in which you see the bird. Is it wading in a saltwater marsh? Walking along a riverbank or on the beach? Soaring in the sky? Is it perched high in the trees or hopping along the forest floor? Because of their preferences in diet and habitat, you'll usually see robins hopping on the ground, but not often eating seeds at a feeder. Or you will see a Blue Jay sitting on the branches of a tree, but not climbing headfirst down a tree trunk like the Brown-headed Nuthatch.

Noticing what a bird is eating will give you another clue to help you identify that bird. Feeding is a big part of any bird's life. Fully one-third of all bird activity revolves around searching for and catching food, or actually eating. While birds don't always follow all the rules of what we think they eat, you can make some general assumptions. Northern Flickers, for instance, feed upon ants and other insects, so you wouldn't expect to see them visiting a backyard feeder. Some birds, such as Barn Swallows and Tree Swallows, feed upon flying insects, and spend hours swooping and diving to catch a meal.

Sometimes you can identify a bird by the way it perches. Body posture can help you differentiate between an American Crow and a Red-tailed Hawk. American Crows lean forward over their feet on a branch, while hawks perch in a vertical position. Look for this the next time you see a large unidentified bird in a tree.

Birds in flight are often difficult to identify, but noting the size and shape of the wing will help. A bird's wing size is in direct proportion to its body size, weight and type of flying. The shape of the wing determines if the bird flies fast and with precision, or slowly and less precisely. Birds such as House Finches, which flit around in thick tangles of branches, have short round wings. Birds that soar on warm updrafts of air, such as Turkey Vultures, have long broad wings. Barn Swallows have short pointed wings that slice through air, propelling their swift and accurate flight.

Some birds have unique flight patterns that aid in identification. American Goldfinches fly in a distinctive up-and-down pattern that makes it look as if they are riding a roller coaster.

While it's not easy to make these observations in the short time you often have to watch a "mystery bird," practicing these methods of identification will greatly expand your skills in birding. Also, seek the guidance of a more experienced birder who will help you improve your skills and answer questions on the spot.

BIRD BASICS

It's easier to identify birds and communicate about them if you know the names of the different parts of a bird. For instance, it's more effective to use the word "crest" to indicate the set of extra long feathers on top of a Northern Cardinal's head than to try to describe it.

The following illustration points out the basic parts of a bird. Because it is a composite of many birds, it shouldn't be confused with any actual bird.

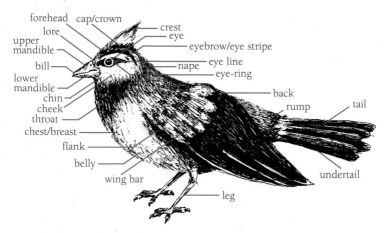

BIRD COLOR VARIABLES

No other animal has a color pallet like a bird's. Brilliant blues, lemon yellows, showy reds and iridescent greens are common-place within the bird world. In general, the male birds are more colorful than their female counterparts. This is probably to help the male attract a mate, essentially saying, "Hey, look at me!" It also calls attention to the male's overall health. The better the condition of his feathers, the better his food source and territory, and therefore, the better his potential for a mate.

Female birds that don't look like their male counterparts (such species are called sexually dimorphic, meaning "two forms") are often a nondescript color, as seen with the Boat-tailed Grackle. These muted tones help to hide the females during weeks of motionless incubation, and draw less attention to them when they are out feeding or taking a break from the rigors of raising their young.

In some species, such as the Bald Eagle, Blue Jay and Downy Woodpecker, the male birds look nearly identical to the females. In the case of the woodpeckers, the sexes are only differentiated by a single red or sometimes yellow mark. Depending on the species, the mark may be on top of the head, face, nape of the neck or just behind the bill.

During the first year, juvenile birds often look like the mothers. Since brightly colored feathers are used mainly for attracting a mate, young non-breeding males don't have a need for colorful plumage. It is not until the first spring molt (or several years later, depending on the species) that young males obtain their breeding colors.

Both breeding and winter plumages are the result of molting. Molting is the process of dropping old worn feathers and replacing them with new ones. All birds molt, typically twice a year, with the spring molt usually occurring in late winter. During this time, most birds produce their breeding plumage (brighter colors for attracting mates), which lasts throughout the summer.

Winter plumage is the result of the late summer molt, which serves a couple of important functions. First, it adds feathers for warmth in the coming winter. Second, in some species it produces feathers that tend to be drab in color, which helps to camouflage the birds and hide them from predators. The winter plumage of the male American Goldfinch, for example, is an olive brown, unlike its obvious canary yellow color in summer. Luckily for us, some birds, such as the male Northern Cardinal, retain their bright summer colors all year long.

BIRD NESTS

Bird nests are truly an amazing feat of engineering. Imagine building your home strong enough to weather a storm, large enough to hold your entire family, insulated enough to shelter them from cold and heat, and waterproof enough to keep out rain. Now, build it without any blueprints or directions, and without the use of your hands or feet! Birds do!

Before building a nest, an appropriate site must be selected. In some species, such as House Wrens, the male picks out several potential sites and assembles several small twigs in each. This discourages other birds from using nearby nest cavities. These "extra" nests are occasionally called dummy nests. The female is then taken around and shown all the choices. She chooses her favorite and finishes constructing the nest. In some other species of birds—Baltimore Orioles, for example—it is the female who chooses the site and builds the nest with the male offering only an occasional suggestion. Each species has its own nest-building routine, which is strictly followed.

Nesting material usually consists of natural elements found in the immediate area. Most nests consist of plant fibers (such as bark peeled from grapevines), sticks, mud, dried grass, feathers, fur, or soft fuzzy tufts from thistle. Some birds, including Ruby-throated Hummingbirds, use spider webs to glue nest materials together. Nesting material is limited to what a bird can hold or carry. Because of this, a bird must make many trips afield to gather enough materials to complete its nest. Most nests take at least four days or more, and hundreds, if not thousands, of trips to build.

As you'll see in the following illustrations, birds build a wide variety of nest types.

ground nest   platform nest   cup nest   pendulous nest

The simple **ground nest** is scraped out of the earth. A shallow depression that usually contains no nesting material, it is made by birds such as the Killdeer and Black Skimmer.

Another kind of nest, the **platform nest**, represents a more complex type of nest building. Constructed of small twigs and branches, the platform nest is a simple arrangement of sticks which forms a platform and features a small depression to nestle the eggs.

Some platform nests, such as those of the Common Loon, are constructed on the ground, and are made of mud and grass. Platform nests can also be on cliffs, bridges, balconies or even in flowerpots. This kind of nest gives space to adventurous youngsters, and functions as a landing platform for the parents. Many waterfowl construct platform nests on the ground, usually near water or actually in the water. These floating platform nests vary with the water level, thus preventing nests with eggs from being flooded. Platform nests, constructed by such birds as Mourning Doves and herons, are not anchored to the tree, and may tumble from the branches during high winds and storms.

The **cup nest** is a modified platform nest, used by three-quarters of all songbirds. Constructed from the outside in, a supporting platform is constructed first. This platform is attached firmly to a tree, shrub or rock ledge. Next, the sides are constructed of grasses, small twigs, bark or leaves, which are woven together and often glued with mud for additional strength. The inner cup, lined with feathers, animal fur, soft plant material or animal hair, is constructed last. The mother bird uses her chest to cast the final contours of the inner nest.

The **pendulous nest** is an unusual nest, looking more like a sock hanging from a branch than a nest. Inaccessible to most predators, these nests are attached to the ends of the smallest branches of a tree, and often wave wildly in the breeze. Woven very tightly of plant fibers, they are strong and watertight, taking up to a week to build. More commonly used by tropical birds, this complicated nest type has also been mastered by orioles and kinglets. A small opening on the top or side allows the parents access to the grass-lined interior. (It must be one heck of a ride to be inside one of these nests during a windy spring thunderstorm!)

One of the most clever of all nest types is known as the **no nest** or daycare nest. Parasitic birds, such as Brown-headed Cowbirds, build no nests at all! The egg-laden female expertly searches out other birds' nests and sneaks in to lay one of her own eggs while the host mother is not looking, thereby leaving the host mother to raise an adopted youngster. The mother cowbird wastes no energy building a nest only to have it raided by a predator. By using several nests of other birds, she spreads out her progeny in hope that at least one of her offspring will live to maturity.

Another type of nest, the **cavity nest**, is used by many birds, including woodpeckers and Eastern Bluebirds. The cavity nest is usually excavated in a tree branch or trunk, and offers shelter from storms, sun, predators and cold. A relatively small entrance hole in a tree leads to an inner chamber up to 10 inches (25 cm) below. Usually constructed by woodpeckers, the cavity nest is typically used only once by its builder, but subsequently can be used for many years by birds such as Wood Ducks, mergansers and bluebirds, which do not have the capability of excavating one for themselves. Kingfishers, on the other hand, excavate a tunnel up to 4 feet (1 m) long, which connects the entrance in a riverbank to the nest chamber. These cavity nests are often sparsely lined because they are already well insulated.

Some birds, including some swallows, take nest building one step further. They use a collection of small balls of mud to construct an adobe-style home. Constructed beneath the eaves of houses, under bridges or inside chimneys, some of these nests look like simple cup nests. Others are completely enclosed, with small tunnel-like openings that lead into a safe nesting chamber for the baby birds.

WHO BUILDS THE NEST?

In general, the female bird builds the nest. She gathers nesting materials and constructs a nest, with an occasional visit from her mate to check on the progress. In some species, both parents contribute equally to the construction of a nest. A male bird might forage for precisely the right sticks, grass or mud, but it's often the female that forms or puts together the nest. She uses her body to form the egg chamber. Rarely does the male build a nest by himself.

FLEDGING

Fledging is the interval between hatching and flight or leaving the nest. Some birds leave the nest within hours of hatching (precocial), but it might be weeks before they are able to fly. This is common with waterfowl and shorebirds. Until they start to fly, they are called fledglings. Birds that are still in the nest are called nestlings. Other baby birds are born naked and blind, and remain in the nest for several weeks (altricial).

WHY BIRDS MIGRATE

Why do birds migrate? The short answer is simple—food. Birds migrate to areas with high concentrations of food, as it is easier to breed where food is than where it is not. A typical migrating bird—the Summer Tanager, for instance—will migrate from the tropics of Central and South America to nest in the forests of North America, taking advantage of billions of newly hatched insects to feed its young. This trip is called **complete migration**.

Some birds of prey return from their complete migration to northern regions that are overflowing with small rodents, such as mice and voles, that have continued to breed in winter.

Complete migrators have a set time and pattern of migration. Each year at nearly the same time, they take off and head for a specific wintering ground. Complete migrators may travel great distances, sometimes as much as 15,000 miles (24,150 km) or more in a year. But complete migration doesn't necessarily imply flying from the cold, frozen northland to a tropical destination. The Dark-eyed Junco, for example, is a complete migrator that flies from the far reaches of Canada to spend the winter right here in Virginia.

There are many interesting aspects to complete migrators. In the spring, males usually migrate several weeks before the females, arriving early to scope out possibilities for nesting sites and food sources, and to begin to defend territories. The females arrive several weeks later. In the autumn, in many species, the females and their young leave early, often up to four weeks before the adult males.

All migrators are not the same type. There are **partial migrators**, such as American Goldfinches, that usually wait until the food supply dwindles before flying south. Unlike complete migrators, the partial migrators move only far enough south, or sometimes east and west, to find abundant food. In some years it might be only a few hundred miles, while in other years it might be nearly a thousand. This kind of migration, dependent on the weather and available food, is sometimes called **seasonal movement**.

Unlike the predictable ebbing and flowing behavior of complete migrators or partial migrators, **irruptive migrators** can move every third to fifth year or, in some cases, in consecutive years. These migrations are triggered when times are really tough and food is scarce. Red-breasted Nuthatches are a good example of irruptive migrators, because they leave their normal northern range in search of food or in response to overpopulation.

How Do Birds Migrate?

One of the many secrets of migration is fat. While we humans are fighting the battle of the bulge, birds intentionally gorge themselves to put on as much fat as possible while still being able to fly. Fat provides the greatest amount of energy per unit of weight, and in the same way that your car needs gas, birds are propelled by fat and stalled without it.

During long migratory flights, fat deposits are used up quickly, and birds need to stop to "refuel." This is when backyard bird feeding stations and undeveloped, natural spaces around our towns and cities are especially important. Some birds require up to two to three days of constant feeding to build up their fat reserves before continuing their seasonal trip.

Some birds, such as most eagles, hawks, ospreys, falcons and vultures, migrate during the day. Larger birds can hold more body fat, go longer without eating and take longer to migrate. These birds glide along on rising columns of warm air, called thermals, which hold them aloft while they slowly make their way north or south. They generally rest at night and hunt early in the morning before the sun has a chance to warm up the land and create good soaring conditions. Birds migrating during the day use a combination of landforms, rivers, and the rising and setting sun to guide them in the right direction.

Most other birds migrate during the night. Studies show that some birds which migrate at night use the stars to navigate. Others use the setting sun, while still others, such as doves, use the earth's magnetic fields to guide them north or south. While flying at night might seem like a crazy idea, nocturnal migration is safer for several reasons. First, there are fewer nighttime predators for migrating birds. Second, traveling at night allows time during the day to find food in unfamiliar surroundings. Finally, nighttime wind patterns tend to be flat, or laminar. These flat winds don't have the turbulence associated with the daytime winds, and can actually help carry smaller birds by pushing them along.

HOW TO USE THIS GUIDE

To help you quickly and easily identify birds, this book is organized by color. Simply note the color of the bird and turn to that section. Refer to the first page for the color key. The Red-headed Woodpecker, for example, is black and white with a red head. Because the bird is mostly black and white, it will be found in the black and white section. Each color section is also arranged by size, generally with the smaller birds first. Sections may also incorporate the average size in a range, which, in some cases, reflects size differences between the male and female birds. Flip through the pages in that color section to find the bird. If you already know the name of the bird, check the index for the page number. In some species, the male and female are remarkably different in color. In others, the color of the breeding and winter plumages differs. These species have an inset photograph with a page reference and in most cases are found in two color sections.

In the description section you will find a variety of information about the bird. On the next page is a sample of the information included in the book.

RANGE MAPS

Range maps are included for each bird. Colored areas indicate where in Virginia a particular bird is most likely to be found. Green is used for summer, blue for winter, red for year-round and yellow for areas where the bird is seen during migration. While every effort has been made to accurately depict these ranges, they are only general guidelines. Ranges actually change on an ongoing basis due to a variety of factors. Changes in the weather, species abundance, landscape and vital resources such as the availability of food and water can affect local populations, migration and movements, causing birds to be found in areas not typical for the species.

Colored areas simply mean bird sightings for that species have been frequent in those areas and less frequent in the others. Please use the maps as intended–as general guides only.

COMMON NAME
Scientific name

YEAR-ROUND
MIGRATION
SUMMER
WINTER

Size: measures head to tail, may include wingspan

Male: a brief description of the male bird, and may include breeding, winter or other plumages

Female: a brief description of the female bird, which is sometimes not the same as the male

Juvenile: a brief description of the juvenile bird, which often looks like the female

Nest: the kind of nest this bird builds to raise its young; who builds the nest; how many broods per year

Eggs: how many eggs you might expect to see in a nest; color and marking

Incubation: the average time parents spend incubating the eggs; who does the incubation

Fledging: the average time young spend in the nest after hatching but before they leave the nest; who does the most "childcare" and feeding

Migration: complete (consistent, seasonal), partial migrator (seasonal, destination varies), irruptive (unpredictable, depends on the food supply), non-migrator; additional comments

Food: what the bird eats most of the time (e.g., seeds, insects, fruit, nectar, small mammals, fish); if it typically comes to a bird feeding station

Compare: notes about other birds that look similar, and the pages on which they can be found

Stan's Notes: Interesting gee-whiz natural history information. This could be something to look or listen for, or something to help positively identify the bird. Also includes remarkable features.

1

female
pg. 125

male

EASTERN TOWHEE
Pipilo erythrophthalmus

Size: 7-8" (18-20 cm)

Male: A mostly black bird with dirty red-brown sides and white belly. Long black tail with white tip. Short, stout, pointed bill and rich red eyes. White wing patches flash in flight.

Female: similar to male, but is brown, not black

Juvenile: light brown, a heavily streaked head, chest and belly, long dark tail with white tip

Nest: cup; female builds; 2 broods per year

Eggs: 3-4; creamy white with brown markings

Incubation: 12-13 days; female incubates

Fledging: 10-12 days; male and female feed young

Migration: complete, southern states, South America, non-migrator in parts of Virginia

Food: insects, seeds, fruit; visits ground feeders

Compare: Slightly smaller than the American Robin (pg. 251). The Gray Catbird (pg. 245) lacks a black "hood" and rusty sides. Male Rose-breasted Grosbeak (pg. 33) has a rosy patch on chest. Male Orchard Oriole (pg. 285) is the same size, but unlike ground-dwelling Towhee, is often high in trees.

Stan's Notes: Common name comes from its distinctive "tow-hee" call given by both sexes. Mostly known for its characteristic call that sounds like, "Drink-your-tea!" Seen hopping backward with both feet (bilateral scratching), raking up leaf litter in search of insects and seeds. The female broods, but the male does the most feeding of young. White-eyed form in southern states, red-eyed elsewhere.

3

female pg. 129

male

BROWN-HEADED COWBIRD
Molothrus ater

Size: 7½" (19 cm)

Male: A glossy black bird, reminiscent of a Red-winged Blackbird. Chocolate brown head with a pointed, sharp gray bill.

Female: dull brown bird with bill similar to male

Juvenile: similar to female, only dull gray color and a streaked chest

Nest: no nest; lays eggs in nests of other birds

Eggs: 5-7; white with brown markings

Incubation: 10-13 days; host bird incubates eggs

Fledging: 10-11 days; host birds feed young

Migration: complete, to southern states, non-migrator in Virginia

Food: insects, seeds; will come to seed feeders

Compare: The male Red-winged Blackbird (pg. 9) is slightly larger, with red and yellow patches on upper wings. Common Grackle (pg. 11) has a long tail and lacks the brown head. European Starling (pg. 7) has a shorter tail.

Stan's Notes: A member of the blackbird family. Of approximately 750 species of parasitic birds worldwide, this is the only parasitic bird in Virginia, laying all eggs in host birds' nests, leaving others to raise its young. Cowbirds are known to have laid eggs in nests of over 200 species of birds. Some birds reject cowbird eggs, but most incubate them and raise the young, even to the exclusion of their own. Look for warblers and other birds feeding young birds twice their own size. At one time cowbirds followed bison to feed on insects attracted to the animals.

winter

breeding

EUROPEAN STARLING
Sturnus vulgaris

YEAR-ROUND

Size: 7½" (19 cm)

Male: Gray-to-black bird with white speckles in fall and winter. Shiny purple black during spring and summer. Long, pointed yellow bill in spring turns gray in fall. Short tail.

Female: same as male

Juvenile: similar to adult, gray brown in color with a streaked chest

Nest: cavity; male and female line the cavity; 2 broods per year

Eggs: 4-6; bluish with brown markings

Incubation: 12-14 days; female and male incubate

Fledging: 18-20 days; female and male feed young

Migration: non-migrator to partial migrator; some will move to southern states

Food: insects, seeds, fruit; comes to seed and suet feeders

Compare: Looks similar to Common Grackle (pg. 11), but lacks its long tail.

Stan's Notes: A great songster, this bird can also mimic sounds. Often displaces woodpeckers, chickadees and other cavity-nesting birds. Can be very aggressive and destroy eggs or young of other birds. The bill changes color with the seasons: yellow in spring and gray in autumn. Jaws are designed to be the most powerful when opening, as they pry open crevices to locate hidden insects. Gathers in the hundreds in autumn. Not a native bird, it was introduced to New York City in 1890-91 from Europe.

female pg. 141

male

RED-WINGED BLACKBIRD
Agelaius phoeniceus

YEAR-ROUND

Size: 8½" (22 cm)

Male: Jet black bird with red and yellow shoulder patches on upper wings. Pointed black bill.

Female: heavily streaked brown bird with a pointed brown bill and white eyebrows

Juvenile: same as female

Nest: cup; female builds; 2-3 broods per year

Eggs: 3-4; bluish green with brown markings

Incubation: 10-12 days; female incubates

Fledging: 11-14 days; female and male feed young

Migration: non-migrator to partial migrator in Virginia

Food: seeds, insects; will come to seed feeders

Compare: Slightly larger than the male Brown-headed Cowbird (pg. 5), but is less iridescent and lacks Cowbird's brown head. Differs from all blackbirds due to the red and yellow patches on its wings (epaulets).

Stan's Notes: One of the most widespread and numerous birds in Virginia. It is a sure sign of spring when the Red-winged Blackbirds return to the marshes. Flocks of up to 100,000 birds have been reported. Males return before the females and defend territories by singing from tops of surrounding vegetation. Males repeat call from the tops of cattails while showing off their red and yellow wing bars (epaulets). Females choose mate and usually will nest over shallow water in thick stands of cattails. Red-wingeds feed mostly on seeds in fall and spring, switching to insects during summer.

COMMON GRACKLE
Quiscalus quiscula

Size: 11-13" (28-33 cm)

Male: Large black bird with iridescent blue black head, purple brown body, long black tail, long thin bill and bright golden eyes.

Female: similar to male, only duller and smaller

Juvenile: similar to female

Nest: cup; female builds; 2 broods per year

Eggs: 4-5; greenish white with brown markings

Incubation: 13-14 days; female incubates

Fledging: 16-20 days; female and male feed young

Migration: non-migrator to partial in Virginia; moves around to find food

Food: fruit, seeds, insects; comes to seed feeders

Compare: Male Boat-tailed Grackle (pg. 17) is slightly larger and has a much longer tail. Breeding European Starling (pg. 7) is much smaller, with a speckled appearance and yellow bill. Male Red-winged Blackbird (pg. 9) has red and yellow wing markings.

Stan's Notes: Usually nests in small colonies of up to 75 pairs, but travels with other blackbirds in large flocks. Is known to feed in farmers' fields. Name comes from the Latin word *graculus*, meaning "to cough," for its loud raspy call. Holds its tail in a keel-like position during flight. The flight pattern is almost always level, as opposed to having undulating up-and-down movements. Unlike most birds, has larger muscles to open mouth rather than to close it, as it pries open crevices to locate hidden insects.

COMMON MOORHEN
Gallinula chloropus

Size: 14" (36 cm)

Male: Nearly black overall with yellow-tipped red bill. Red forehead. Thin line of white along sides. Yellowish green legs.

Female: same as male

Juvenile: same as adult, but brown with white throat, legs dirty yellow

Nest: ground; female and male build; 1-2 broods per year

Eggs: 2-10; brown with dark markings

Incubation: 19-22 days; female and male incubate

Fledging: 40-50 days; female and male feed young

Migration: complete, to Florida, Central America and South America

Food: insects, snails, seeds

Compare: Similar size as the American Coot (pg. 15), which lacks the distinctive yellow-tipped bill and red forehead of Moorhen.

Stan's Notes: Also known as Mud Hen or Pond Chicken. A nearly all-black duck-like bird often seen in freshwater marshes and lakes. Walks on floating vegetation or swims while hunting for insects. Females known to lay eggs in other moorhen nests in addition to their own. Sometimes takes old nest in a low shrub. A cooperative breeder, having young of first brood help raise young of second. Young leave nest usually within a few hours after hatching, but stay with the family for a couple months. Young ride on backs of adults.

AMERICAN COOT
Fulica americana

Size: 13-16" (33-40 cm)

Male: Slate gray to black all over, white bill with dark band near tip. Green legs and feet. A small white patch near the base of the tail. Prominent red eyes, with a small red patch above bill between eyes.

Female: same as male

Juvenile: much paler than adult, with a gray bill and same white rump patch

Nest: floating platform; female and male build; 1 brood per year

Eggs: 9-12; pinkish buff with brown markings

Incubation: 21-25 days; female and male incubate

Fledging: 49-52 days; female and male feed young

Migration: complete, to southern states, Mexico and Central America; winters in Virginia

Food: insects, aquatic plants

Compare: Smaller than most waterfowl, it is the only black water bird or duck-like bird with a white bill.

Stan's Notes: An excellent diver and swimmer, often seen in large flocks on open water. Not a duck, as it doesn't have webbed feet, but instead has large lobed toes. When taking off, scrambles across surface of water with wings flapping. Bobs head while swimming. Nest is floating mat of vegetation. Huge flocks of up to 1,000 birds gather for fall migration and during winter. The unusual name is of unknown origin, but in Middle English, *coote* was used to describe various waterfowl–perhaps it stuck. Also called Mud Hen.

15

female pg. 167

male

BOAT-TAILED GRACKLE
Quiscalus major

Size: 16" (40 cm), male
14" (36 cm), female

Male: Iridescent blue-black bird with a very long keel-shaped tail. Bright yellow eyes.

Female: brown version of male, lacks iridescence

Juvenile: similar to female

Nest: cup; female builds; 2 broods per year

Eggs: 2-4; pale greenish blue, brown markings

Incubation: 13-15 days; female incubates

Fledging: 12-15 days; female feeds young

Migration: non-migrator; moves around to find food

Food: insects, berries, seeds, fish; visits feeders

Compare: Similar to male Common Grackle (pg. 11), but male Boat-tailed has a distinctive long tail. Similar size as the Fish Crow (pg. 19) and American Crow (pg. 21), but a very different shape. Look for an iridescent blue head and a very long tail.

Stan's Notes: A noisy bird of coastal saltwater and inland marshes, giving several harsh, high-pitched calls and several squeaks. Eats a wide variety of foods from grains to fish. Sometimes seen picking insects off the backs of cattle. Will also visit bird feeders. Makes a cup nest with mud or cow dung and grass. Nests in small colonies. Most nesting occurs from April through May. Boat-taileds on the Atlantic coast have bright yellow eyes, while the Gulf coast birds have dark eyes.

17

FISH CROW
Corvus ossifragus

YEAR-ROUND

Size: 16" (40 cm)

Male: All-black bird appearing nearly identical to the American Crow, but with a longer tail, and smaller head and bill.

Female: same as male

Juvenile: same as adult

Nest: cup; female and male build; 1 brood a year

Eggs: 4-5; blue or gray-green, brown markings

Incubation: 16-18 days; female and male incubate

Fledging: 21-24 days; female and male feed young

Migration: non-migrator

Food: aquatic insects, carrion, mollusks, berries, seeds

Compare: Nearly identical to American Crow (pg. 21), but the Fish Crow is smaller, has a longer tail, and a smaller head and bill. Fish Crow is most easily differentiated from American Crow by its higher-pitched call.

Stan's Notes: Essentially a bird of the coast and along major rivers, but can be found inland in Virginia. Not uncommon for it to break open mollusk shells by dropping them on rocks from above. Very sociable and gregarious. Nests in small colonies, often building a stick nest halfway up a tree. Forms small winter flocks of up to 100 birds, unlike the American Crow, which often forms winter flocks of several hundred. The best way to distinguish between the two crow species is by their remarkably different calls. Fish Crow has a high, nasal "cah."

19

AMERICAN CROW
Corvus brachyrhynchos

Size: 18" (45 cm)

Male: All-black bird with black bill, legs and feet. Can have a purple sheen in direct sunlight.

Female: same as male

Juvenile: same as adult

Nest: platform; female builds; 1 brood per year

Eggs: 4-6; bluish to olive green, brown markings

Incubation: 18 days; female incubates

Fledging: 28-35 days; female and male feed young

Migration: non-migrator

Food: fruit, insects, mammals, fish, carrion; will come to seed and suet feeders

Compare: Nearly identical to the Fish Crow (pg. 19), but American Crow is larger, has a shorter tail, and a larger head and bill. American Crow is most easily differentiated from Fish Crow by its lower-pitched call.

Stan's Notes: This is one of the most recognizable birds in Virginia. Often reuses its nest every year if not taken over by a Great Horned Owl. Collects and stores bright, shiny objects in the nest. Able to mimic human voices, and other birds. One of the smartest of all birds and very social, often entertaining itself by provoking chases with other birds. Feeds on road kill but is rarely hit by cars. Can live up to 20 years. Unmated birds, known as helpers, help raise young. Large extended families roost together at night, dispersing during the day to hunt.

soaring

BLACK VULTURE
Coragyps atratus

Size: 25" (63 cm); up to 4¾-foot wingspan

Male: Black vulture with dark gray head and legs. Short tail. In flight, all black with light gray wing tips, and feet extending beyond tail.

Female: same as male

Juvenile: similar to adult

Nest: no nest on a stump or on ground, or takes abandoned nest; 1 brood per year

Eggs: 2; light green with dark markings

Incubation: 37-48 days; female and male incubate

Fledging: 80-90 days; female and male feed young

Migration: non-migrator

Food: dead animals, occasionally captures small live mammals

Compare: Slightly smaller than the Turkey Vulture (pg. 25), lacking Turkey Vulture's bright red head. Turkey Vulture has two-toned wings, a black leading edge and light gray trailing edge. Black Vulture has shorter wings and tail than the Turkey Vulture.

Stan's Notes: Also called Black Buzzard. A more gregarious bird than the Turkey Vulture. In flight, the Black Vulture holds its wings straight out to its sides, unlike the Turkey Vulture which holds its wings in a V pattern. More aggressive while feeding but less skilled at finding carrion, it is thought Black Vulture's sense of smell is less developed than Turkey Vulture's. Families stay together for up to a year. Often nests and roosts with other Black Vultures. If startled, especially at the nest, it regurgitates with power and accuracy.

23

soaring

TURKEY VULTURE
Cathartes aura

YEAR-ROUND

Size: 26-32" (66-80 cm); up to 6-foot wingspan

Male: Large bird with obvious red head and legs. In flight, the wings appear two-toned: black leading edge with gray on the trailing edge and tip. The tips of wings end in finger-like projections. Long squared tail. Ivory bill.

Female: same as male

Juvenile: similar to adult, with gray-to-blackish head and bill

Nest: no nest, or minimal nest on cliff or in cave; 1 brood per year

Eggs: 2; white with brown markings

Incubation: 38-41 days; female and male incubate

Fledging: 66-88 days; female and male feed young

Migration: complete, to southern states, Mexico, and Central and South America, non-migrator in Virginia

Food: carrion; parents regurgitate for young

Compare: Slightly larger than Black Vulture (pg. 23) and has longer wings and tail. Flies holding wings in a slight V shape, unlike the Black Vulture's straight wing position.

Stan's Notes: The vulture's naked head is an adaptation to reduce risk of feather fouling (picking up diseases) from carcasses. Unlike hawks and eagles, it has weak feet more suited to walking than grasping. One of the few birds that has a developed sense of smell. Mostly mute, making only grunts and groans. Seen in trees with wings outstretched to catch sun.

drying

DOUBLE-CRESTED CORMORANT
Phalacrocorax auritus

Size: 33" (84 cm)

Male: Large all-black water bird with long snake-like neck. A long yellow orange bill with a hooked tip.

Female: same as male

Juvenile: lighter brown with a grayish-colored breast and neck

Nest: platform, in colony; male and female build; 1 brood per year

Eggs: 3-4; bluish white without markings

Incubation: 25-29 days; female and male incubate

Fledging: 37-42 days; male and female feed young

Migration: complete, to southern coastal states, Mexico and Central America, non-migrator along coastal Virginia

Food: small fish, aquatic insects

Compare: Similar size as the Turkey Vulture (pg. 25), which also perches on branches with wings open to dry in sun, but Vulture has a naked red head. Twice the size of American Coot (pg. 15), which lacks the Cormorant's long neck and long pointed bill.

Stan's Notes: Often seen flying in large V formation. Often roosts in large groups in trees near water. Catches fish by swimming with wings held at its sides. To dry off it strikes an erect pose with wings outstretched, facing the sun. The name refers to its nearly invisible crests. "Cormorant" comes from the Latin *corvus*, meaning "crow," and *L. marinus*, meaning "pertaining to the sea," literally, "Sea Crow."

BLACK-AND-WHITE WARBLER
Mniotilta varia

Size: 5" (13 cm)

Male: Striped like a zebra, this small warbler has a distinctive black-and-white striped cap. White belly. Black chin and cheek patch.

Female: same as male, only duller and without the black chin and cheek patch

Juvenile: similar to female

Nest: cup; female builds; 1 brood per year

Eggs: 4-5; white with brown markings

Incubation: 10-11 days; female incubates

Fledging: 9-12 days; female and male feed young

Migration: complete, to Florida, Mexico, Central and South America

Food: insects

Compare: Look for Warbler to creep down tree trunks headfirst, like White-breasted and Brown-headed Nuthatches (pp. 219 and 213).

Stan's Notes: The only warbler that moves headfirst down a tree trunk. Look for this common warbler searching for insect eggs in the bark of large trees. Song sounds like a slowly turning, squeaky wheel. Female will perform a distraction dance to draw predators away from the nest. Makes its nest on the ground, concealed under dead leaves or at the base of a tree. A common summer resident, nesting throughout Virginia. More conspicuous during spring and fall migrations. Most arrive in March to April, and leave in October.

male

female

DOWNY WOODPECKER
Picoides pubescens

Size: 6" (15 cm)

Male: A small woodpecker with an all-white belly, black-and-white spotted wings, a black line running through the eyes, a short black bill, a white stripe down the back and red mark on the back of the head. Several small black spots along the sides of white tail.

Female: same as male, but lacks a red mark on head

Juvenile: same as female, some have a red mark near the forehead

Nest: cavity; male and female excavate; 1 brood per year

Eggs: 3-5; white without markings

Incubation: 11-12 days; female and male incubate, the female during day, male at night

Fledging: 20-25 days; male and female feed young

Migration: non-migrator

Food: insects, seeds; visits seed and suet feeders

Compare: Almost identical to the Hairy Woodpecker (pg. 37), but smaller. Look for the shorter, thinner bill of Downy to differentiate them.

Stan's Notes: One of the most abundant and widespread woodpeckers in the state, found throughout where trees are present. Stiff tail feathers help brace this bird like a tripod as it clings to a tree. Like all woodpeckers, has a long barbed tongue for pulling insects from tiny places. Both sexes drum on branches or hollow logs to announce territories that are rarely larger than 5 acres (2 ha). Male performs most of the brooding. Will winter roost in cavity.

female
pg. 123

male

ROSE-BREASTED GROSBEAK
Pheucticus ludovicianus

MIGRATION
SUMMER

Size: 7-8" (18-20 cm)

Male: A plump black-and-white bird with a large, triangular rose patch in the center of chest. Wing linings are rosy red. Large ivory bill.

Female: heavily streaked brown and white bird with large white eyebrows, orange yellow wing linings

Juvenile: same as female

Nest: cup; the female and male build; 1-2 broods per year

Eggs: 3-5; blue green with brown markings

Incubation: 13-14 days; female and male incubate

Fledging: 9-12 days; female and male feed young

Migration: complete, to Mexico, Central America and South America

Food: insects, seeds, fruit; comes to seed feeders

Compare: Male is very distinctive with no look-alikes.

Stan's Notes: Seen during spring and fall migrations. Often prefers mature deciduous forest for nesting, mostly in western Virginia at elevations of 3,000 to 5,000 feet (900 to 1,500 m). Both sexes sing, but the male sings much louder and clearer. Has a rich, robin-like song. The name "Grosbeak" refers to its large bill, used to crush seeds. Rose breast patch varies in size and shape in each male. Late to arrive in spring, early to leave in fall. Males arrive in small groups first, joined by females several days later. Several males can be seen visiting seed feeders at the same time during spring. When females arrive, males become territorial and reduce their visits to feeders. Young grosbeaks visit feeders with adults after fledging.

male

female

YELLOW-BELLIED SAPSUCKER
Sphyrapicus varius

MIGRATION
SUMMER
WINTER

Size: 8-9" (20-22.5 cm)

Male: Medium-sized woodpecker with checkered back. Has a red forehead, crown and chin. Tan-to-yellow breast and belly. White wing patches flash while flying.

Female: similar to male, white chin

Juvenile: similar to female, dull brown and lacks any red marking

Nest: cavity; female and male excavate; 1 brood per year

Eggs: 5-6; white without markings

Incubation: 12-13 days; female and male incubate, the female during day, male at night

Fledging: 25-29 days; female and male feed young

Migration: complete, to southern states, Mexico and Central America; winters in Virginia

Food: insects, tree sap; comes to suet feeders

Compare: The male Yellow-bellied Sapsucker shares the red chin of Red-headed Woodpecker (pg. 39), but lacks an all-red head. Female Yellow-bellied Sapsucker has a white chin.

Stan's Notes: Drills holes in a pattern of horizontal rows in small- to medium-sized trees to bleed tree sap. Many birds drink from sapsucker taps. Oozing sap also attracts insects, which sapsuckers eat. Sapsuckers will defend their sapping sites from the other birds. They don't suck sap; rather, they lap it with their long tongues. A quiet bird with few vocalizations, but will mew like a cat. Unlike other woodpeckers, drumming rhythm is irregular.

35

male

female

HAIRY WOODPECKER
Picoides villosus

Size: 9" (22.5 cm)

Male: Black-and-white woodpecker with a white belly, and black wings with rows of white spots. White stripe down back. Long black bill. Red mark on back of head.

Female: same as male, but lacks a red mark on head

Juvenile: grayer version of female

Nest: cavity; female and male excavate; 1 brood per year

Eggs: 3-6; white without markings

Incubation: 11-15 days; female and male incubate, the female during day, male at night

Fledging: 28-30 days; male and female feed young

Migration: non-migrator

Food: insects, nuts, seeds; comes to seed and suet feeders

Compare: Larger than Downy Woodpecker (pg. 31), Hairy has a longer bill and lacks Downy's black spots along tail.

Stan's Notes: A common backyard bird that announces its arrival with a sharp chirp before landing on feeders. Barbed tongue helps extract insects from trees. Responsible for eating many destructive forest insects. Has tiny bristle-like feathers at base of bill to protect the nostrils from wood dust. Will drum on hollow logs, branche or stovepipes in springtime to announce its territory. Often prefe to excavate nest cavities in live aspen trees. Has a larger, more ov shaped cavity entrance than that of Downy Woodpecker.

YEAR-ROUND

RED-HEADED WOODPECKER
Melanerpes erythrocephalus

Size: 9" (22.5 cm)

Male: All-red head and a solid black back. White rump, chest and belly. Large white patches on wings flash when in flight. A black tail. Gray legs and bill.

Female: same as male

Juvenile: gray brown with white chest, lacks any red

Nest: cavity; male builds with help from female; 1 brood per year

Eggs: 4-5; white without markings

Incubation: 12-13 days; female and male incubate

Fledging: 27-30 days; female and male feed young

Migration: partial migrator to non-migrator; will move to areas with abundant supply of nuts

Food: insects, nuts, fruit; comes to seed and suet feeders

Compare: No other woodpecker in Virginia has an all-red head. Pileated Woodpecker (pg. 59) is the only other woodpecker that has a solid black back, but it has a partial red head.

Stan's Notes: One of the few woodpecker species in which male and female appear the same (look alike). Bill is not as well adapted for excavating holes as in other woodpeckers, so it chooses dead or rotten tree branches for nest. Later nesting than the closely relate Red-bellied Woodpecker and will often take over its nesting cavi Prefers more open or edge woodland with many dead trees. Of seen perching on tops of dead snags. Stores acorns and other n

male

female

RED-BELLIED WOODPECKER
Melanerpes carolinus

YEAR-ROUND

Size: 9¼" (23 cm)

Male: "Zebra-backed" woodpecker with a white rump. Red crown extends down the nape of neck. Tan breast with a tinge of red on belly, which is often hard to see.

Female: same as male, but with a gray crown

Juvenile: gray version of adults, no red cap or nape

Nest: cavity; the female and male build; 1 brood per year

Eggs: 4-5; white without markings

Incubation: 12-14 days; female and male incubate, the female during day, male at night

Fledging: 24-27 days; female and male feed young

Migration: non-migrator

Food: insects, nuts, fruit; comes to seed and suet feeders

Compare: Similar to Northern Flicker (pg. 157) and Yellow-bellied Sapsucker (pg. 35). Note the tan chest and belly with obvious black-and-white stripes on the back. The Red-headed Woodpecker (pg. 39) has an all-red head.

Stan's Notes: Named for its easily overlooked rosy red belly patch. Mostly a bird of shady woodland, it excavates holes in rotten wood looking for spiders, centipedes and beetles. Hammers acorns and berries into crevices of trees for winter food. Will return to same tree to excavate a new nest below that of the previous year. Often kicked out of nest hole by European Starlings.

winter

breeding

RUDDY TURNSTONE
Arenaria interpres

MIGRATION
WINTER

Size: 9½" (24 cm)

Male: Breeding has orange legs, a black and white head marking, black bib, white breast and belly, black and chestnut wings and back. Slightly upturned black bill. Winter has a brown and white head and breast pattern.

Female: similar to male, only duller

Juvenile: similar to adults, but black and white head has a scaly appearance

Nest: ground; female builds; 1 brood per year

Eggs: 3-4; olive green with dark markings

Incubation: 22-24 days; male and female incubate

Fledging: 19-21 days; male feeds young

Migration: complete, to coastal Virginia and southern coastal states, South America

Food: aquatic insects, fish, mollusks, crustaceans, worms, eggs

Compare: Unusually ornamented shorebird. Look for a striking black and white pattern on head and neck, and orange legs to identify.

Stan's Notes: Most common in the winter. Also called Rock Plover. Named "Turnstone" because it turns stones over on rocky beaches to find food. Known for its unusual behavior of robbing and eating other birds' eggs. Hangs around crabbing operations to eat scraps from nets. Can be very tolerant of humans when feeding. Female often leave before the young leave nests (fledge), resulting in th males raising young. Males have a bare spot on the belly (bro patch) to warm the young, something only females normally h

winter pg. 257

breeding

BLACK-BELLIED PLOVER
Pluvialis squatarola

MIGRATION
WINTER

Size: 11-12" (28-30 cm)

Male: Striking black and white breeding plumage. Black belly, face, neck, chest and sides. A white cap, nape of neck and belly near tail. Black legs and bill.

Female: less black on chest and belly than male

Juvenile: grayer than adults, with much less black

Nest: ground; the male and female build; 1 brood per year

Eggs: 3-4; pinkish or greenish with black-brown markings

Incubation: 26-27 days; male and female incubate, the male during day, female at night

Fledging: 35-45 days; male feeds young, young learn quickly to feed themselves

Migration: complete, to the East and Gulf coasts, West Indies and coastal South America

Food: insects

Compare: The breeding Dunlin (pg. 137) is slightly smaller, with a rusty back and long down-curved bill. Look for extensive black patch on belly, face and chest, and a white cap.

Stan's Notes: The males perform a "butterfly" courtship flight to attract females. Female leaves male and young about 12 days after eggs hatch. Breeds at age 3. Arrivals start in July and August (fall migration), and leaves in April. Doesn't breed here. In flight, in any plumage, displays white rump and stripe on wings with black axillaries (armpits). Often darts over ground to grab an insect and run.

45

BLACK-NECKED STILT
Himantopus mexicanus

Size: 14" (36 cm)

Male: Upper parts of the head, neck and back are black. Lower parts are white. Ridiculously long red-to-pink legs. Long black bill.

Female: similar to male, only browner on back

Juvenile: similar to female, brown instead of black

Nest: ground; the female and male build; 1 brood per year

Eggs: 3-5; off-white with dark markings

Incubation: 22-26 days; female and male incubate

Fledging: 28-32 days; female and male feed young

Migration: complete, to South America

Food: aquatic insects

Compare: Outrageous length of the red-to-pink legs make this shorebird hard to confuse with any other.

Stan's Notes: A summer resident in Virginia, found along the East coast and as far north as the Great Lakes. A bird of shallow freshwater and saltwater marches. Very vocal, giving a "kek-kek-kek" call. Nests solitarily or in small colonies in open areas above the tide line. Known for transporting water with water-soaked belly feathers (belly-soaking) to cool eggs during hot weather.

female pg. 173

male

LESSER SCAUP
Aythya affinis

Size: 16-17" (40-43 cm)

Male: Appears mostly black with bold white sides and gray back. Chest and head look nearly black, but head appears purple with green highlights in direct sun. Bright yellow eyes.

Female: overall brown with dull white patch at base of light gray bill, yellow eyes

Juvenile: same as female

Nest: ground; female builds; 1 brood per year

Eggs: 8-14; olive buff without markings

Incubation: 22-28 days; female incubates

Fledging: 45-50 days; female teaches young to feed

Migration: complete, Virginia, southern states, Mexico, Central America, northern South America

Food: aquatic plants and insects

Compare: The male Ring-necked Duck (pg. 51) has a bold white ring around its bill and a black back, compared with male Lesser Scaup's gray back. Male Ring-necked lacks the bold white sides of the male Lesser Scaup.

Stan's Notes: A common wintering duck in Virginia, completely submerging itself to feed on the bottom of lakes, unlike dabbling ducks which only tip forward to reach bottom. Often seen in large flocks on lakes, ponds and sewage lagoons during migration and winter. When seen in flight, note the bold white stripe under the wings. An interesting baby-sitting arrangement in which groups of young are tended by one to three adult females. Prefers fresh water, but can be seen along the coast. Doesn't breed in Virginia.

female pg. 179

male

RING-NECKED DUCK
Aythya collaris

Size: 17" (43 cm)

Male: A striking duck with black head, chest and back. Sides are gray to nearly white. Has a bold white ring around the bill and second ring at base of bill. Top of head is peaked.

Female: dark brown back, light brown sides, a gray face, dark brown crown, white line behind eyes and white ring around the bill, top of head peaked

Juvenile: similar to female

Nest: ground; female builds; 1 brood per year

Eggs: 8-10; olive gray to brown without markings

Incubation: 26-27 days; female incubates

Fledging: 49-56 days; female teaches young to feed

Migration: complete, to Virginia, southern states, West Indies, Mexico and Central America

Food: aquatic plants and insects

Compare: Similar size as male Lesser Scaup (pg. 49), which has a gray back, compared with the black back of the male Ring-necked Duck. Look for the male Ring-necked's prominent white ring around the bill.

Stan's Notes: A common wintering duck in Virginia. Usually seen in larger freshwater lakes rather than saltwater marshes. A diving duck, watch for it to dive underwater to forage for food. Takes to flight by springing up off water. Named "Ring-necked" because of the cinnamon-colored collar (nearly impossible to see in the field). Also known as Ring-billed Duck due to obvious white ring on bill

female pg. 183

male

WINTER

HOODED MERGANSER
Lophodytes cucullatus

Size: 16-19" (40-48 cm)

Male: A sleek black-and-white bird that has rusty brown sides. Crest "hood" raises to reveal a large white patch. Long, thin black bill.

Female: sleek brown and rust bird with a ragged rusty crest and long, thin brown bill

Juvenile: similar to female

Nest: cavity; female lines old woodpecker hole; 1 brood per year

Eggs: 10-12; white without markings

Incubation: 32-33 days; female incubates

Fledging: 71 days; female feeds young

Migration: complete, to coastal states and Mexico

Food: small fish, aquatic insects

Compare: A distinctive diving bird, look for the male's large white patch "hood" on the head and rusty brown sides. Similar size as the male Wood Duck (pg. 275), but lacking the green head of Wood Duck.

Stan's Notes: A small diving bird of shallow-water ponds, sloughs, lakes and rivers. The male Hooded Merganser can voluntarily raise and lower its crest to show off the large white head patch. Rarely is found away from wooded areas, where it nests in natural cavities or nest boxes. Female will "dump" eggs into other female Hooded Merganser nests, resulting in 20 to 25 eggs in some nests. Often associated with Wood Ducks, this bird has been known to share a nest cavity with a Wood Duck, sitting side by side. A winter visitor that doesn't nest in Virginia.

skimming

BLACK SKIMMER
Rynchops niger

YEAR-ROUND
SUMMER

Size: 18" (45 cm); up to 3½-foot wingspan

Male: A striking black and white bird with black on top and white on bottom. Very distinct black-tipped red bill with lower bill longer than the upper. Red legs tuck up and out of sight when in flight.

Female: similar to male, only smaller

Juvenile: similar to adults, spotty brown on top

Nest: ground; the female and male build; 1 brood per year

Eggs: 3-5; bluish white with brown markings

Incubation: 21-23 days; female and male incubate

Fledging: 23-25 days; female and male feed young

Migration: complete, to South America, partial to non-migrator along coastal Virginia

Food: small fish, shrimp

Compare: Similar shape as Royal Tern (pg. 303), but lacks the black back and black-tipped red bill of Black Skimmer. No other large black and white bird skims across the water like Black Skimmer. In addition, no other bird has a lower bill longer than the upper bill.

Stan's Notes: Also called Scissorbill or Razorbill, referring to this bird's unusual, long bill. Uses its unique bill while in flight to cut through the water surface to catch fish or shrimp near the surface. Commonly feeds with several other skimmers. Often seen flying to and from nesting colony with fish in its bill. Nests in large colonies, often associated with tern species. Found along the East coast.

AMERICAN OYSTERCATCHER
Haematopus palliatus

Size: 18-19" (45-48 cm)

Male: A large shorebird with large red-orange bill, black head, and dark brown sides, wings and back. White chest and belly, pink legs and a red ring around the eyes.

Female: same as male

Juvenile: more gray than black and lacks the brightly colored bill

Nest: ground; the male and female build; 1 brood per year

Eggs: 2-4; olive with sparse brown markings

Incubation: 24-29 days; male and female incubate, the male during day, female at night

Fledging: 35-40 days; male and female feed young, young learn quickly to feed themselves

Migration: complete, to the West Indies, East, Gulf and South American coasts, partial migrator on the Virginia coast

Food: shellfish, insects, aquatic insects, worms

Compare: Larger than breeding Black-bellied Plover (pg. 45). Look for the large and obvious red-orange bill of Oystercatcher to identify.

Stan's Notes: This large, chunky shorebird has a flattened, heavy bill, which it uses to pry open shellfish and probe sand for insects and worms. Can be categorized according to its preferred oyster-opening technique. Stabbers sneak up on mollusks and stab their bills between shells before they have a chance to close. Hammerers shatter one-half of the shell with several direct, powerful blows.

male

female

PILEATED WOODPECKER
Dryocopus pileatus

Size: 19" (48 cm)

Male: Crow-sized woodpecker with a black back and bright red crest. Long gray bill with red mustache. White leading edge of the wings flashes brightly when flying.

Female: same as male, but has a black forehead and lacks red mustache

Juvenile: similar to adults, only duller and browner

Nest: cavity; male and female excavate; 1 brood per year

Eggs: 3-5; white without markings

Incubation: 15-18 days; female and male incubate, the female during day, male at night

Fledging: 26-28 days; female and male feed young

Migration: non-migrator

Food: insects; will come to suet feeders

Compare: Red-headed Woodpecker (pg. 39) is about half the size, and has an all-red head, black back and white rump. Look for the bright red crest and exceptionally large size of the Pileated Woodpecker.

Stan's Notes: Our largest woodpecker. The common name comes from the Latin *pileatus*, which means "wearing a cap," referring to its crest. Relatively shy bird that prefers large tracts of woodland. Drums on hollow branches, chimneys, etc., to announce territory. Excavates oval holes up to several feet long in tree trunks, looking for insects to eat. Large chips of wood lay at bases of excavated trees. Favorite food is carpenter ants. Young are fed regurgitated insects.

BLACK-CROWNED NIGHT-HERON
Nycticorax nycticorax

YEAR-ROUND
MIGRATION
SUMMER

Size: 22-27" (56-69 cm)

Male: A stocky, hunched and inactive heron with black back and crown, white belly and gray wings. Long dark bill, short yellow legs and bright red eyes. Breeding adult has two long white plumes on crown.

Female: same as male

Juvenile: golden brown head and back with white spots, streaked breast, yellow orange eyes, brown bill

Nest: platform; female and male build; 1 brood per year

Eggs: 3-5; light blue without markings

Incubation: 24-26 days; female and male incubate

Fledging: 42-48 days; female and male feed young

Migration: complete, to southern coastal states, Mexico and Central America

Food: fish, aquatic insects

Compare: Half the size of Great Blue Heron (pg. 271) when perching. Look for a short-necked heron with a black back and crown.

Stan's Notes: A very secretive bird, this heron is most active near dawn and dusk (crepuscular). It hunts alone, but nests in small colonies. Roosts in trees during the day. Often squawks if disturbed from the daytime roost. Often seen being harassed by other herons during days.

61

soaring

OSPREY
Pandion haliaetus

Size: 24" (60 cm); up to 5½-foot wingspan

Male: Large eagle-like bird with a white chest and belly, and a nearly black back. White head with a black streak through the eyes. Large wings with black "wrist" marks. Dark bill.

Female: same as male, but larger, with a necklace of brown streaking

Juvenile: similar to adults, with a light tan breast

Nest: platform, often on raised wooden platform; female and male build; 1 brood per year

Eggs: 2-4; white with brown markings

Incubation: 32-42 days; female and male incubate

Fledging: 48-58 days; male and female feed young

Migration: complete, to southern coastal states, Mexico, Central and South America

Food: fish

Compare: Bald Eagle (pg. 67) is on average 10 inches (25 cm) larger, with an all-white head and tail. The juvenile Bald Eagle is brown with white speckles. Look for a white belly and dark stripe through eyes to identify Osprey.

Stan's Notes: Ospreys are in a family all their own. It is the only raptor that plunges into water feet first to catch fish. Can hover for a few seconds before diving. Carries fish in a head-first position for better aerodynamics. Often harassed by Bald Eagles for its catch. In flight, wings are angled (cocked) backward. Nests on man-made towers and in tall dead trees. Recent studies show male and female might mate for life, but don't migrate to same wintering grounds.

winter

breeding

COMMON LOON
Gavia immer

Size: 28-36" (71-90 cm)

Male: Large, familiar black-and-white bird of the lakes. The breeding adult has checkerboard back with white necklace, black head and deep red eyes with long, pointed black bill. Winter has an entirely gray body and bill.

Female: same as male

Juvenile: similar to winter adult, lacks red eyes

Nest: platform, on the ground; female and male build; 1 brood per year

Eggs: 2; olive brown, occasionally brown markings

Incubation: 26-31 days; female and male incubate

Fledging: 75-80 days; female and male feed young

Migration: complete, to East and Gulf coasts, Mexico

Food: fish, aquatic insects

Compare: Double-crested Cormorant (pg. 27) has a yellow bill and black chest.

Stan's Notes: A winter resident on the coast beginning in October, lasting until March. Some non-breeding adults remain all summer. Prefers clear lakes because it hunts for fish by eyesight. Legs are set so far back that it has a hard time walking on land, but it is a great swimmer. Name comes from the Swedish *lom*, meaning "lame," for the awkward way it walks on land. Its unique call suggests the wild laughter of a demented person, and led to the phrase "crazy as a loon." Young ride on backs of swimming parents. Adults perform distraction displays to protect young. Very sensitive to disturbance during nesting and will abandon nest.

soaring

juvenile

BALD EAGLE
Haliaeetus leucocephalus

Size: 31-37" (79-94 cm); up to 7-foot wingspan

Male: Pure white head and tail contrast with dark brown-to-black body and wings. A large, curved yellow bill and yellow feet.

Female: same as male, only slightly larger

Juvenile: dark brown with white spots or speckles throughout body and wings, gray bill

Nest: massive platform, usually in a tree; female and male build; 1 brood per year

Eggs: 2; off-white without markings

Incubation: 34-36 days; female and male incubate

Fledging: 75-90 days; female and male feed young

Migration: partial migrator, to southeastern states

Food: fish, carrion, birds (mainly ducks)

Compare: Larger than the Black Vulture (pg. 23) and Turkey Vulture (pg. 25). Black Vulture has a shorter tail and lacks adult Bald Eagle's white head and tail. Turkey Vulture flies with its two-toned wings held in a V, unlike the straight-out wing position of Eagle.

Stan's Notes: Driven to near extinction due to DDT poisoning and illegal killing. Now making a comeback in North America. Returns to same nest each year, adding more sticks, enlarging it to massive proportions, at times up to 1,000 pounds (450 kg). In the midair mating ritual, one eagle will flip upside down and lock talons with another. Both tumble, then break apart to continue flight. Thought to mate for life, but will switch mates if not successful reproducing. Juvenile attains the white head and tail at about 4 to 5 years of age.

BLUE-GRAY GNATCATCHER
Polioptila caerulea

SUMMER

Size: 4" (10 cm)

Male: Light blue head, back and wings, and white chest. Long black tail with white undertail, often held cocked above the rest of body. Black eyebrows. Prominent white eye-ring.

Female: same as male, only grayer

Juvenile: similar to female

Nest: cup; female and male build; 1 brood a year

Eggs: 4-5; pale blue with dark markings

Incubation: 10-13 days; female and male incubate

Fledging: 10-12 days; female and male feed young

Migration: complete, to southern states, the Bahamas, Mexico and Central America

Food: insects

Compare: The only small blue bird with a black tail. Constantly flicks its tail up and down and from side to side. Very active near the nest, look for it flitting around upper branches in search of insects.

Stan's Notes: Found in a wide variety of forest types throughout Virginia. Listen for its wheezy call notes to help locate. A fun and easy bird to watch as it cocks and fans tail while calling. In many years, it nests so early that by mid-June it is no longer defending territory. Like many other open woodland nesters, it is a common cowbird host. Although population is abundant and widespread, it has been decreasing in the recent past.

female pg. 103

male

INDIGO BUNTING
Passerina cyanea

Size: 5½" (14 cm)

Male: Vibrant blue finch-like bird. Scattered dark markings on wings and tail.

Female: light brown bird with faint markings

Juvenile: similar to female

Nest: cup; female builds; 2 broods per year

Eggs: 3-4; pale blue without markings

Incubation: 12-13 days; female incubates

Fledging: 10-11 days; female feeds young

Migration: complete, to Mexico, Central America and South America

Food: insects, seeds, fruit; will visit seed feeders

Compare: Smaller than male Eastern Bluebird (pg. 77) and male Blue Grosbeak (pg. 79). Lacks the Bluebird's rusty red breast, and Grosbeak's chestnut-colored wing bars and large bill.

Stan's Notes: Usually only the males are noticed. Actually a black bird, as it doesn't have any blue pigment in its feathers. As with the Blue Jay, sunlight is refracted within the structure of the bunting's feathers, making them appear blue. Appears iridescent in direct sun. Molts to acquire body feathers with gray tips, which quickly wear off to reveal bright blue plumage in spring. Molts in fall to appear like females during winter. Males often sing from treetops to attract mates. Will come to feeders in spring before insects are plentiful. Mostly seen along woodland edges, feeding on insects. Migrates at night in flocks of five to ten birds. A late migrant, males return before females and juveniles, usually returning to previous year's nest site. Juveniles move to within a mile from birth site.

TREE SWALLOW
Tachycineta bicolor

Size: 5-6" (13-15 cm)

Male: Blue green in the spring and greener in fall. Appears to change color in direct sunlight. A white belly, a notched tail and pointed wing tips.

Female: similar to male, only duller

Juvenile: gray brown with a white belly and grayish breast band

Nest: cavity; female and male line former woodpecker cavity or nest box; 1 brood per year

Eggs: 4-6; white without markings

Incubation: 13-16 days; female incubates

Fledging: 20-24 days; female and male feed young

Migration: complete, to coastal Virginia and southern coastal states, Mexico, Central America

Food: insects

Compare: Similar color to Purple Martin (pg. 81), but smaller and has white chest and belly. Barn Swallow (pg. 75) has rust belly and deeply forked tail.

Stan's Notes: This swallow is most common along coastal beaches, freshwater ponds and lakes, and agricultural fields. Attracted to your yard with a nesting box. Competes with Eastern Bluebirds for cavities and nest boxes. Will travel great distances to find dropped feathers to line its grass nest. Sometimes seen playing, chasing after dropped feathers. It is often seen flying back and forth across open fields, feeding on insects. Gathers in large flocks to migrate.

BARN SWALLOW
Hirundo rustica

SUMMER

Size:	7" (18 cm)
Male:	A sleek swallow with a blue black back, a cinnamon belly and a reddish brown chin. White spots on long forked tail.
Female:	same as male, only slightly duller
Juvenile:	similar to adults, with a tan belly and chin, and shorter tail
Nest:	cup; female and male build; 2 broods a year
Eggs:	4-5; white with brown markings
Incubation:	13-17 days; female incubates
Fledging:	18-23 days; female and male feed young
Migration:	complete, to South America
Food:	insects, prefers beetles, wasps and flies
Compare:	Tree Swallow (pg. 73) has a white belly and chin, and notched tail. The Chimney Swift (pg. 91) has narrow pointed tail with wings longer than the body. The Purple Martin (pg. 81) is nearly 2 inches (5 cm) larger and has a dark purple belly.

Stan's Notes: Of the six swallow species in Virginia, this is the only one with a deeply forked tail. Unlike other swallows, the Barn Swallow rarely glides in flight, so look for continuous flapping. It builds a mud nest using up to 1,000 beak-loads of mud, often in or on barns. Nests in colonies of four to six, but nesting alone is not uncommon. Drinks while flying by skimming water or getting water from wet leaves. It also bathes while flying through the rain or sprinklers.

male

female

EASTERN BLUEBIRD
Sialia sialis

YEAR-ROUND

Size: 7" (18 cm)

Male: Reminiscent of its larger cousin, American Robin, with a rusty red breast and a white belly. Sky blue head, back and tail.

Female: shares rusty red breast and white belly, but is grayer with faint blue tail and wings

Juvenile: similar to female, with spots on chest, blue wing markings

Nest: cavity, old woodpecker cavity or man-made nest box; female builds; 2 broods per year

Eggs: 4-5; pale blue without markings

Incubation: 12-14 days; female incubates

Fledging: 15-18 days; male and female feed young

Migration: partial migrator to non-migrator in Virginia

Food: insects, fruit

Compare: Male Indigo Bunting (pg. 71) is nearly all blue, lacking the rusty red breast. Blue Jay (pg. 83) is considerably larger, with a crest and white markings.

Stan's Notes: Year-round resident that is joined by many northern migrants, swelling populations each winter. Once nearly eliminated from Virginia due to a lack of nesting cavities, bluebirds have made a remarkable comeback with the aid of bird enthusiasts who have put up thousands of bluebird boxes. Easily tamed, will come to a shallow dish with mealworms. Bluebirds like open fields, pastures, roadsides and other open habitats. Will perch in trees or on fence posts and wait for grasshoppers. Gives a distinctive "chur-lee chur chur-lee" song. Young of first brood help raise young of second.

female
pg. 121

male

BLUE GROSBEAK
Guiraca caerulea

MIGRATION
SUMMER

Size: 7" (18 cm)

Male: An overall blue bird. Two chestnut-colored wing bars. A large gray-to-silver bill, black around base of bill.

Female: overall brown with darker wings and tail, two tan wing bars, large gray-to-silver bill

Juvenile: similar to female

Nest: cup; female builds; 1-2 broods per year

Eggs: 3-6; pale blue without markings

Incubation: 11-12 days; female incubates

Fledging: 9-10 days; female and male feed young

Migration: complete, to the Bahamas, Cuba, Mexico and Central America

Food: insects, seeds; will come to seed feeders

Compare: The male Indigo Bunting (pg. 71) is very similar, but is smaller and more common than the male Blue Grosbeak. Look for two chestnut wing bars and a large heavy bill to distinguish it from the male Bunting.

Stan's Notes: A common summer resident, Blue Grosbeaks return to Virginia by mid-April and leave in October. A bird of semi-open habitats such as overgrown fields, riversides, woodland edges and fencerows. Visits seed feeders, where it is often confused with male Indigo Buntings. Often seen twitching and spreading its tail. First-year males show only some blue, obtaining the full complement of blue feathers in the second winter.

PURPLE MARTIN
Progne subis

Size: 8½" (22 cm)

Male: A large swallow-shaped bird with a purple head, back and belly. Black wings and tail. Notched tail.

Female: gray purple head and back with a whitish belly, darker wings and tail

Juvenile: same as female

Nest: cavity; female and male line the cavity of house; 1 brood per year

Eggs: 4-5; white without markings

Incubation: 15-18 days; female incubates

Fledging: 26-30 days; male and female feed young

Migration: complete, to South America

Food: insects

Compare: The male is the only swallow with a dark purple belly. Usually only seen in groups.

Stan's Notes: Largest swallow species in North America. Used to nest in tree cavities in Virginia, but now nearly exclusively nests in man-made nesting boxes. Its main diet consists of dragonflies, not mosquitoes as once thought. Often drinks and bathes while flying by skimming water or flying through rain. Returns to the same nest site each year. Males arrive before the females and yearlings. Often nests within 100 feet (30 m) of a human dwelling and, in fact, the most successful colonies are located within this distance. Young strike out to form new colonies. Huge colonies gather in autumn to migrate to South America.

BLUE JAY
Cyanocitta cristata

Size: 12" (30 cm)

Male: Large bright-light-blue and white bird with black necklace. Crest moves up and down at will. White face with a gray belly. White wing bars on blue wings. Black spots and a white tip on blue tail.

Female: same as male

Juvenile: same as adult, only duller

Nest: cup; the female and male build; 1-2 broods per year

Eggs: 4-5; green to blue with brown markings

Incubation: 16-18 days; female incubates

Fledging: 17-21 days; female and male feed young

Migration: non-migrator to partial migrator; will move around to find abundant food source

Food: insects, fruit, carrion, seeds, nuts; comes to seed feeders, and ground feeders with corn

Compare: Eastern Bluebird (pg. 77) is much smaller and lacks the crest. The Belted Kingfisher (pg. 85) lacks the vivid blue coloring and black necklace of Blue Jay.

Stan's Notes: Highly intelligent bird, solving problems, gathering food and communicating more than other birds. Will scream like a hawk to scatter birds at a feeder before approaching. Known as the alarm of the forest, screaming at any intruders in the woods. Is known to eat eggs or young birds from nests of other birds. One of the few birds to cache food. Feathers don't contain blue pigment; refracted sunlight casts blue light.

male

female

BELTED KINGFISHER
Ceryle alcyon

Size: 13" (33 cm)

Male: Large blue bird with white belly. Broad blue gray breast band and a ragged crest that is raised and lowered at will. Large head with a long, thick black bill. A small white spot directly in front of red brown eyes. Black wing tips with splashes of white that flash when flying.

Female: same as male, but with rusty breast band in addition to blue gray band, and rusty flanks

Juvenile: similar to female

Nest: cavity; female and male excavate; 1 brood per year

Eggs: 6-7; white without markings

Incubation: 23-24 days; female and male incubate

Fledging: 23-24 days; female and male feed young

Migration: complete, to southern states, Central and South America, non-migrator in Virginia

Food: small fish

Compare: Similar in size to the Blue Jay (pg. 83), but the Kingfisher is darker blue with a larger, more ragged crest.

Stan's Notes: Seen perched on branches near the water, it dives headfirst for small fish and returns to a branch to eat. Has a loud machine-gun-like call. Excavates a deep cavity in bank of river or lake. Parents drop dead fish into water, teaching the young to dive. Regurgitates pellets of bone after meals, being unable to pass bones through digestive tract. Mates recognize each other by call.

non-breeding adult

white juvenile

breeding

molting juvenile

LITTLE BLUE HERON
Egretta caerulea

YEAR-ROUND
MIGRATION
SUMMER

Size: 24" (60 cm)

Male: Dark slate blue to purple nearly all year. Breeding has several long plumes on crown with a reddish purple head and neck. Dull green legs, feet. Black-tipped blue-gray bill.

Female: same as male

Juvenile: pure white overall, yellowish legs and feet, black-tipped gray bill

Nest: platform; female and male build; 1 brood per year

Eggs: 2-6; light blue without markings

Incubation: 20-23 days; female and male incubate

Fledging: 42-49 days; female and male feed young

Migration: complete, to Central and South America, partial to non-migrator in coastal Virginia

Food: fish, aquatic insects

Compare: Breeding adult lacks Tricolored's (pg. 89) white belly. Juvenile is confused with the Snowy Egret (pg. 307), which has bright yellow feet, black legs and solid black bill. Breeding Cattle Egret (pg. 305) has orange buff crest, breast and back, red-orange bill.

Stan's Notes: A coastal resident, although much less numerous in winter. Unusual because the young look completely different from adults. All-white young turn blotchy white in the first year. By the second year they look like the adult birds. A very slow stalker of prey, feeding in freshwater lakes and rivers, saltwater marshes and wetlands. Nests in large colonies near saltwater sites.

TRICOLORED HERON
Egretta tricolor

YEAR-ROUND

Size: 26" (66 cm)

Male: Dark blue head, neck and wings contrast with a white belly and neck. Small brown patches at base of neck with lighter brown on lower back. A long, slender yellow bill with a dark tip. Legs yellow to pale green.

Female: same as male

Juvenile: similar to adult, chestnut brown in place of dark blue areas

Nest: platform; female and male build; 1 brood per year

Eggs: 3-6; light blue without markings

Incubation: 21-25 days; female and male incubate

Fledging: 32-35 days; female and male feed young

Migration: non-migrator to partial migrator in Virginia

Food: fish, aquatic insects

Compare: Great Blue Heron (pg. 271) is much larger and lacks white undersides. The Little Blue Heron (pg. 87) is slightly smaller and lacks the Tricolored's yellow bill and white belly.

Stan's Notes: A medium-sized heron characterized by its white undersides. Like other herons, Tricolored has declined in numbers due to wetland habitat loss. To hunt, it stands still and waits. Will also chase after small fish. A year-round resident, although much less numerous in the winter. Seen mainly in saltwater marshes and estuaries, but also in freshwater marshes inland. Known to wander as far as Kansas. Colony nester with other herons, one adult always on duty at the nest. Was not hunted for plumes like other herons.

SUMMER

CHIMNEY SWIFT
Chaetura pelagica

Size: 5" (13 cm)

Male: Nondescript, swallow-shaped bird, usually only seen flying. Long, thin all-brown body with a pointed tail and head. Long swept-back wings are longer than body.

Female: same as male

Juvenile: same as adult

Nest: half cup; female and male build; 1 brood per year

Eggs: 4-5; white without markings

Incubation: 19-21 days; female and male incubate

Fledging: 28-30 days; female and male feed young

Migration: complete, to South America

Food: insects caught in air

Compare: Considerably smaller than Purple Martin (pg. 81) and lacks the iridescent purple of the Martin. Barn Swallow (pg. 75) has a forked tail, compared with the pointed tail of Chimney Swift. Tree Swallow (pg. 73) has a white belly and blue green back.

Stan's Notes: One of the fastest fliers in the bird world. Spends all day flying, rarely perching. Bathes and drinks by skimming across water surfaces. Unique in-flight twittering call is often heard before bird is seen. Flies in groups, feeding on flying insects nearly 100 feet (30 m) in the air. Often called Flying Cigar due to its pointed body shape. Hundreds will nest and roost in large chimneys, hence the common name. Builds nest with tiny twigs, cementing it with saliva, attaching it to inside of chimney or hollow tree.

CHIPPING SPARROW
Spizella passerina

Size: 5" (13 cm)

Male: Small gray brown sparrow with a clear gray chest, rusty crown, white eyebrows with a black eye line, thin gray black bill and two faint wing bars.

Female: same as male

Juvenile: similar to adult, has a streaked breast, lacks the rusty crown

Nest: cup; female builds; 2 broods per year

Eggs: 3-5; blue green with brown markings

Incubation: 11-14 days; female incubates

Fledging: 10-12 days; female and male feed young

Migration: complete, to southern states, Mexico and Central America, non-migrator in Virginia

Food: insects, seeds; will come to ground feeders

Compare: Smaller than the Song Sparrow (pg. 107), which has a heavily streaked chest. Female House Finch (pg. 97) also has a streaked chest, compared with the unmarked chest of Chipping Sparrow.

Stan's Notes: Year-round resident in Virginia and common garden or yard bird, often seen feeding on dropped seeds beneath feeders. In northern states, gathers in large family groups in autumn to feed in preparation for migration. Migrates at night in flocks of 20 to 30 birds. Received its common name from the male's slow "chip" call. Often just called Chippy. Nest is placed low in dense shrubs and is almost always lined with animal hair.

PINE SISKIN
Carduelis pinus

Size: 5" (13 cm)

Male: Small brown finch. Heavily streaked back, breast and belly. Yellow wing bars. Yellow at base of tail. Thin bill.

Female: same as male

Juvenile: similar to adult, light yellow tinge over the breast and chin

Nest: modified cup; the female builds; 2 broods per year

Eggs: 3-4; greenish blue with brown markings

Incubation: 12-13 days; female incubates

Fledging: 14-15 days; female and male feed young

Migration: irruptive; moves around the state in search of food

Food: seeds, insects; will come to seed feeders

Compare: Female American Goldfinch (pg. 319) lacks streaks and has white wing bars. Female House Finch (pg. 97) has a streaked chest, but lacks yellow wing bars. Female Purple Finch (pg. 111) has bold white eyebrows.

Stan's Notes: Usually considered a winter finch, seen in flocks of up to 20 individuals, often with other finch species. While it can be found throughout Virginia in heavy invasion years, it is absent in many winters. Travels and breeds in small groups. Comes to thistle feeders. Male feeds female during incubation. Juveniles lose yellow tint by late summer of first year. Builds nest toward ends of coniferous branches, where needles are dense, helping to conceal. Nests are often only a few feet apart. Doesn't nest in Virginia.

male pg. 287

female

HOUSE FINCH
Carpodacus mexicanus

YEAR-ROUND

Size: 5" (13 cm)

Female: A plain brown bird with a heavily streaked white chest.

Male: orange red face, chest and rump, a brown cap, brown marking behind eyes, brown wings streaked with white, streaked belly

Juvenile: similar to female

Nest: cup, sometimes in cavities; female builds; 2 broods per year

Eggs: 4-5; pale blue, lightly marked

Incubation: 12-14 days; female incubates

Fledging: 15-19 days; female and male feed young

Migration: non-migrator to partial migrator; will move around to find food

Food: seeds, fruit, leaf buds; will visit seed feeders

Compare: The female Purple Finch (pg. 111) is very similar, but has bold white eyebrows. The female American Goldfinch (pg. 319) has a clear chest and white wing bars. Similar to Pine Siskin (pg. 95), but lacks yellow wing bars and has a much larger bill than Siskin.

Stan's Notes: Very social bird. Visits feeders in small flocks. Likes nesting in hanging flower baskets. Incubating female is fed by the male. Has a loud, cheerful warbling song. House Finches originally introduced to Long Island, New York, from the western U.S. in the 1940s have since populated the entire eastern U.S. Now found all over the country. Suffers from a fatal eye disease that causes eyes to crust over.

HOUSE WREN
Troglodytes aedon

SUMMER

Size: 5" (13 cm)

Male: A small all-brown bird with lighter brown markings on tail and wings. Slightly curved brown bill. Often holds its tail erect.

Female: same as male

Juvenile: same as adult

Nest: cavity; female and male line just about any cavity, 2 broods per year

Eggs: 4-6; tan with brown markings

Incubation: 10-13 days; female and male incubate

Fledging: 12-15 days; female and male feed young

Migration: complete, to southern states and Mexico

Food: insects

Compare: House Wren is distinguished from Carolina Wren (pg. 101) by lack of eyebrow mark. Wren's long curved bill and long upturned tail differentiates it from sparrows.

Stan's Notes: A prolific songster, it will sing from dawn until dusk during the mating season. Easily attracted to nest boxes. In spring, the male chooses several prospective nesting cavities and places a few small twigs in each. Female inspects each, chooses one, and finishes the nest building. She will completely fill the nest cavity with uniformly small twigs, then line a small depression at back of cavity with pine needles and grass. Often has trouble fitting long twigs through nest cavity hole. Tries many different directions and approaches until successful.

CAROLINA WREN
Thryothorus ludovicianus

YEAR-ROUND

Size: 5½" (14 cm)

Male: Warm rusty brown head and back with an orange yellow chest and belly. White throat and a prominent white eye stripe. A short stubby tail, often cocked up.

Female: same as male

Juvenile: same as adult

Nest: cavity; female and male build; 2 broods per year, sometimes 3

Eggs: 4-6; white, sometimes pink or creamy, with brown markings

Incubation: 12-14 days; female incubates

Fledging: 12-14 days; female and male feed young

Migration: non-migrator

Food: insects, fruit, few seeds

Compare: Similar to the House Wren (pg. 99), but the Carolina Wren is lighter brown and has a prominent white eye stripe.

Stan's Notes: Year-round resident in Virginia. Mates are long-term, remaining together throughout the year in permanent territories. Will sing throughout the year. The male is known to sing up to 40 different song types, singing one song repeatedly before switching to another. Female also sings, resulting in duets. Male often takes over feeding the first brood of young while the female renests. The range expands northward in years with mild winters. Will nest in birdhouses, unusual places such as mailboxes, bumpers of cars or broken taillights, or just about any other cavity. Found in brushy yards or woodlands.

female

male pg. 71

INDIGO BUNTING
Passerina cyanea

Size: 5½" (14 cm)

Female: Light brown finch-like bird. Faint streaking on a light tan chest. Wings have a very faint blue cast with indistinct wing bars.

Male: vibrant blue finch-like bird, scattered dark markings on wings and tail

Juvenile: similar to female

Nest: cup; female builds; 2 broods per year

Eggs: 3-4; pale blue without markings

Incubation: 12-13 days; female incubates

Fledging: 10-11 days; female feeds young

Migration: complete, to Mexico, Central America and South America

Food: insects, seeds, fruit; will visit seed feeders

Compare: The female Blue Grosbeak (pg. 121) is larger and has two tan wing bars. Female Indigo Bunting is similar to female finches. Female American Goldfinch (pg. 319) has white wing bars. Female Purple Finch (pg. 111) has white eyebrows and a heavily streaked chest. Female House Finch (pg. 97) also has a heavily streaked chest.

Stan's Notes: A secretive bird, usually only the male buntings are seen. Males often sing from treetops to attract mates. Will come to feeders in the spring before insects are plentiful. Mostly seen along woodland edges, feeding on insects. Migrates at night in flocks of five to ten birds. A late migrant, males return before females and juveniles. Juveniles move to within a mile from birth site.

male pg. 225

female

DARK-EYED JUNCO
Junco hyemalis

Size: 5½" (14 cm)

Female: A round, dark-eyed bird with tan-to-brown chest, head and back. White belly. Ivory-to-pink bill. Since the outermost tail feathers are white, tail appears as a white V in flight.

Male: same as female, only slate gray to charcoal

Juvenile: similar to female, but has a streaked breast and head

Nest: cup; female and male build; 2 broods a year

Eggs: 3-5; white with reddish brown markings

Incubation: 12-13 days; female incubates

Fledging: 10-13 days; male and female feed young

Migration: complete, throughout the U.S.; winters in Virginia

Food: seeds, insects; will come to seed feeders

Compare: Rarely confused with any other bird. Large flocks feed under bird feeders in winter.

Stan's Notes: A common winter bird of Virginia. Usually seen on the ground in small flocks. Migrates from Canada to Virginia and beyond. Males tend to migrate farther south than females. Adheres to a rigid social hierarchy, with the dominant birds chasing the less dominant birds. Look for white outer tail feathers flashing while it's in flight. Most comfortable on the ground, juncos will use both feet to "double-scratch," exposing seeds and insects. Consumes many weed seeds. Several junco species have now been combined into one, simply called Dark-eyed Junco. Nests in western Virginia.

SONG SPARROW
Melospiza melodia

Size: 5-6" (13-15 cm)

Male: Common brown sparrow with heavy dark streaks on breast coalescing into a central dark spot.

Female: same as male

Juvenile: similar to adult, finely streaked breast without a central spot

Nest: cup; female builds; 2 broods per year

Eggs: 3-4; pale blue to green with reddish brown markings

Incubation: 12-14 days; female incubates

Fledging: 9-12 days; female and male feed young

Migration: complete, to Virginia and southern states, non-migrator in Virginia

Food: insects, seeds; rarely visits seed feeders

Compare: Similar to other brown sparrows. Look for a heavily streaked chest with central dark spot.

Stan's Notes: Many Song Sparrow subspecies or varieties, but dark central spot carries through each variant. While the female builds another nest for a second brood, the male sparrow often takes over feeding the young. Returns to a similar area each year, defending a small territory by singing from thick shrubs. A common host of the Brown-headed Cowbird. Ground feeders, look for them to scratch simultaneously with both feet to expose seeds. Unlike many other sparrow species, Song Sparrows rarely flock together.

HOUSE SPARROW
Passer domesticus

Size: 6" (15 cm)

Male: Medium sparrow-like bird with large black spot on throat extending down to the chest. Brown back and single white wing bars. A gray belly and crown.

Female: all-light-brown bird, slightly smaller, lacks the black throat patch and single wing bars

Juvenile: similar to female

Nest: domed cup nest, within cavity; female and male build; 2-3 broods per year

Eggs: 4-6; white with brown markings

Incubation: 10-12 days; female incubates

Fledging: 14-17 days; female and male feed young

Migration: non-migrator; moves around to find food

Food: seeds, insects, fruit; comes to seed feeders

Compare: Lacks the rusty crown of Chipping Sparrow (pg. 93). Look for male House Sparrow's black bib. Female has a clear chest and no marking on head (cap).

Stan's Notes: One of the first bird songs heard in cities in spring. Familiar city bird, nearly always in flocks. Introduced from Europe to Central Park, New York, in 1850 and now found throughout North America. These birds are not really sparrows, but members of the Weaver Finch family, characterized by their large, oversized domed nests. Constructs a nest containing scraps of plastic, paper and whatever else is available. An aggressive bird that will kill the young of other birds in order to take over a cavity.

male pg. 289

female

PURPLE FINCH
Carpodacus purpureus

Size: 6" (15 cm)

Female: A brown bird with a heavily streaked white chest. Prominent white eyebrows.

Male: raspberry red head, cap, breast, back and rump, brownish wings and tail

Juvenile: same as female

Nest: cup; female and male build; 1 brood a year

Eggs: 4-5; greenish blue with brown markings

Incubation: 12-13 days; female incubates

Fledging: 13-14 days; female and male feed young

Migration: irruptive; moves around in search of food

Food: seeds, insects, fruit; comes to seed feeders

Compare: Female House Finch (pg. 97) lacks female Purple Finch's white eyebrows. Pine Siskin (pg. 95) has yellow wing bars and a much smaller bill than Purple Finch. The female American Goldfinch (pg. 319) has a clear chest and white wing bars.

Stan's Notes: Usually only seen in the winter, when Purple Finches leave their northern homes and move around, searching for food. Travels in flocks of up to 50. It is common in non-residential areas (prefers open woods or woodland edges), and has been replaced in cities by House Finches. Feeds primarily on seeds, with ash tree seeds a very important food source. Will visit seed feeders along with House Finches, making it hard to tell them apart. A rich loud song, with a distinctive "tic" note made only in flight. Not a purple color, the Latin species name *purpureus* means "crimson" or other reddish color.

winter pg. 229

breeding

LEAST SANDPIPER
Calidris minutilla

MIGRATION
WINTER

Size: 6" (15 cm)

Male: Breeding adult has golden brown head and back, and white eyebrows. White belly. Dull yellow legs. Short, down-curved black bill.

Female: same as male

Juvenile: similar to winter adult, but buff brown and lacking the breast band

Nest: ground; the male and female build; 1 brood per year

Eggs: 3-4; olive with dark markings

Incubation: 19-23 days; male and female incubate

Fledging: 25-28 days; male and female feed young

Migration: complete, to coastal Virginia and southern coastal states, Central America

Food: insects, aquatic insects, seeds

Compare: The smallest of sandpipers. Often confused with breeding Western Sandpiper (pg. 115) and Semipalmated Sandpiper (pg. 231), Least Sandpiper's yellow legs differentiate it from other tiny sandpipers. The short, thin, down-curved bill also helps to identify.

Stan's Notes: Seen during migration throughout Virginia. Winters in southern coastal states from Virginia to California. The smallest of peeps (sandpipers) that nest on the tundra in northern parts of Canada and Alaska. Its yellow legs can be difficult to see in water, poor light or if covered with mud. Prefers the grassy flats of both saltwater and freshwater ponds. This is a tame sandpiper that can be approached without scaring.

winter pg. 233

breeding

WESTERN SANDPIPER
Calidris mauri

Size: 6½" (16 cm)

Male: Breeding has a bright rust brown crown, ear patch and back with white chin and chest. Black legs. Narrow bill that droops near tip.

Female: same as male

Juvenile: similar to breeding adult, bright buff brown on back only

Nest: ground; the male and female build; 1 brood per year

Eggs: 2-4; light brown with dark markings

Incubation: 20-22 days; male and female incubate

Fledging: 19-21 days; male and female feed young

Migration: complete, to coastal Virginia and southern coastal states, Central America

Food: insects, aquatic insects

Compare: Is often confused with the breeding Least Sandpiper (pg. 113) and the Semipalmated Sandpiper (pg. 231), but bright rust brown crown, ear patch and back help to identify. Look for black legs to differentiate from the Least Sandpiper. Western has a longer bill that droops slightly at tip.

Stan's Notes: A winter resident in southern coastal states from Virginia to California. Nests on the ground in large "loose" colonies on the tundra of northern coastal Alaska. Adults leave breeding grounds several weeks before young. Some obtain their breeding plumage before leaving Virginia in spring. Feeds in deeper water than the Semipalmated Sandpiper.

1

white-striped

tan-striped

WHITE-THROATED SPARROW
Zonotrichia albicollis

WINTER

Size: 6-7" (15-18 cm)

Male: A brown bird with gray tan chest and belly. Small yellow spot between the eyes (lore). Distinctive white or tan throat patch. White or tan stripes alternate with black stripes on crown. Color of the throat patch and crown stripes match.

Female: same as male

Juvenile: similar to adult, gray throat and eyebrows with heavily streaked chest

Nest: cup; female builds; 1 brood per year

Eggs: 4-6; color varies from greenish to bluish to creamy white with red brown markings

Incubation: 11-14 days; female incubates

Fledging: 10-12 days; female and male feed young

Migration: complete, Virginia, southern states, Mexico

Food: insects, seeds, fruit; visits ground feeders

Compare: The Song Sparrow (pg. 107) is smaller, has a central dark spot on the breast and lacks White-throated's black-and-white or black-and-tan striped pattern on the head.

Stan's Notes: There are two color variations (polymorphic) of the White-throated Sparrow: white-striped or tan-striped. Studies have indicated the white-striped adults tend to mate with the tan-striped birds. No indication why. A winter resident that is more abundant during migration, when it can be seen at ground feeders. Nests are built on the ground underneath small trees in bogs and coniferous forests. Doesn't nest in Virginia.

1

MIGRATION
WINTER

SEMIPALMATED PLOVER
Charadrius semipalmatus

Size: 7" (18 cm)

Male: A brown-backed bird with a black necklace and short, black-tipped orange bill. White patch on forehead. White breast and belly. Breeding has a black mask, orange eye-ring.

Female: same as male

Juvenile: similar to adult, lacking well-defined black necklace

Nest: ground; male builds; 1 brood per year

Eggs: 3-4; light brown with dark markings

Incubation: 23-25 days; male and female incubate

Fledging: 22-28 days; male and female feed young

Migration: complete, to coastal Virginia and southern coastal states, Central and South America

Food: insects, seeds, worms

Compare: Smaller than Killdeer (pg. 151) and with only one black necklace, compared with the two of Killdeer. Look for a solid dark back with a very short bill to help identify the Semipalmated Plover.

Stan's Notes: A winter resident in southern coastal states from Virginia to California. This bird is often seen in mixed flocks with Semipalmated Sandpipers. Hunts by running quickly, stopping to look, then stabbing prey. Breeding birds often have orange eye-rings. Prefers to nest in open rocky places, where the male scrapes out a shallow depression. Nests on the ground on the tundra of northern Canada and Alaska.

male pg. 79

female

BLUE GROSBEAK
Guiraca caerulea

Size: 7" (18 cm)

Female: Overall brown with darker wings and tail. Two tan wing bars. Large gray-to-silver bill.

Male: blue bird with two chestnut-colored wing bars, a large gray-to-silver bill with black around base of bill

Juvenile: similar to female

Nest: cup; female builds; 1-2 broods per year

Eggs: 3-6; pale blue without markings

Incubation: 11-12 days; female incubates

Fledging: 9-10 days; female and male feed young

Migration: complete, to the Bahamas, Cuba, Mexico and Central America

Food: insects, seeds; will come to seed feeders

Compare: The female Indigo Bunting (pg. 103) is very similar, but is smaller and more common than the female Blue Grosbeak. The female Bunting lacks the Grosbeak's wing bars and large bill.

Stan's Notes: A common summer resident, Blue Grosbeaks return to Virginia by mid-April and leave in October. A bird of semi-open habitats such as overgrown fields, riversides, woodland edges and fencerows. Visits seed feeders, where it's often confused with female Indigo Buntings. Often seen twitching and spreading its tail. First-year males show only some blue, obtaining the full complement of blue feathers in the second winter.

female

male pg. 33

ROSE-BREASTED GROSBEAK
Pheucticus ludovicianus

MIGRATION
SUMMER

Size: 7-8" (18-20 cm)

Female: Plump, heavily streaked brown and white bird with obvious white eyebrows. Orange yellow wing linings.

Male: black-and-white bird with large, triangular rose patch in center of chest, wing linings rosy red, large ivory bill

Juvenile: same as female

Nest: cup; the female and male build; 1-2 broods per year

Eggs: 3-5; blue green with brown markings

Incubation: 13-14 days; female and male incubate

Fledging: 9-12 days; female and male feed young

Migration: complete, to Mexico, Central America and South America

Food: insects, seeds, fruit; comes to seed feeders

Compare: Female looks like a large sparrow. Female is larger and has a more distinctive eyebrow mark than female Purple Finch (pg. 111). The female House Finch (pg. 97) has no eyebrow mark.

Stan's Notes: Seen during spring and fall migrations. Often prefers mature deciduous forest for nesting, mostly in western Virginia at elevations of 3,000 to 5,000 feet (900 to 1,500 m). Both sexes sing, but the male sings much louder and clearer. "Grosbeak" refers to its large bill, used to crush seeds. Late to arrive in spring, early to leave in fall. Males arrive in small groups first, females arrive several days later. When females arrive, males reduce visits to feeders.

male pg. 3

female

EASTERN TOWHEE
Pipilo erythrophthalmus

YEAR-ROUND
SUMMER

Size: 7-8" (18-20 cm)

Female: A mostly light brown bird. Rusty red brown sides and white belly. Long brown tail with white tip. Short, stout, pointed bill and rich red eyes. White wing patches flash in flight.

Male: similar to female, but is black, not brown

Juvenile: light brown, a heavily streaked head, chest and belly, long dark tail with white tip

Nest: cup; female builds; 2 broods per year

Eggs: 3-4; creamy white with brown markings

Incubation: 12-13 days; female incubates

Fledging: 10-12 days; male and female feed young

Migration: complete, southern states, South America, non-migrator in parts of Virginia

Food: insects, seeds, fruit; visits ground feeders

Compare: Slightly smaller than the American Robin (pg. 251). Female Rose-breasted Grosbeak (pg. 123) has a heavily streaked breast and white eyebrows.

Stan's Notes: Common name comes from its distinctive "tow-hee" call given by both sexes. Mostly known for its characteristic call that sounds like, "Drink-your-tea!" Seen hopping backward with both feet (bilateral scratching), raking up leaf litter in search of insects and seeds. The female broods, but the male does the most feeding of young. White-eyed form in southern states, red-eyed elsewhere.

CEDAR WAXWING
Bombycilla cedrorum

Size: 7½" (19 cm)

Male: Very sleek-looking gray-to-brown bird with pointed crest, light yellow belly and bandit-like black mask. Tip of tail is bright yellow and the tips of wings look as if they have been dipped in red wax.

Female: same as male

Juvenile: slightly smaller, overall gray, lacks red wing tips, black mask and sleek appearance, has a heavily streaked chest

Nest: cup; female and male build; 1 brood a year, occasionally 2

Eggs: 4-6; pale blue with brown markings

Incubation: 10-12 days; female incubates

Fledging: 14-18 days; female and male feed young

Migration: partial migrator; moves around to find food

Food: cedar cones, fruit, insects

Compare: Nearly identical to its larger, less common cousin, Bohemian Waxwing (not shown).

Stan's Notes: The name is derived from its red wax-like wing tips and preference for eating small blueberry-like cones of the cedar. Population increases during winter due to migration. Mostly seen in flocks, moving from area to area, looking for berries. Wanders in winter to find available food supplies. Seen more often in winter because naked branches reveal its presence. In the summer, before berries are abundant, it feeds on insects. Spends most of its time at tops of tall trees. Listen for the very high-pitched "sreee" whistling sounds that it constantly makes.

male pg. 5

female

BROWN-HEADED COWBIRD
Molothrus ater

Size: 7½" (19 cm)

Female: Dull brown bird with no obvious markings. Pointed, sharp gray bill.

Male: glossy black bird, chocolate brown head

Juvenile: similar to female, only dull gray color and a streaked chest

Nest: no nest; lays eggs in nests of other birds

Eggs: 5-7; white with brown markings

Incubation: 10-13 days; host bird incubates eggs

Fledging: 10-11 days; host birds feed young

Migration: complete, to southern states, non-migrator in Virginia

Food: insects, seeds; will come to seed feeders

Compare: Female Red-winged Blackbird (pg. 141) is slightly larger, and has white eyebrows and a streaked chest. European Starling (pg. 7) has speckles and a shorter tail.

Stan's Notes: A member of the blackbird family. Of approximately 750 species of parasitic birds worldwide, this is the only parasitic bird in Virginia, laying all eggs in host birds' nests, leaving others to raise its young. Cowbirds are known to have laid eggs in nests of over 200 species of birds. Some birds reject cowbird eggs, but most incubate them and raise the young, even to the exclusion of their own. Look for warblers and other birds feeding young birds twice their own size. At one time cowbirds followed bison to feed on insects attracted to the animals.

WOOD THRUSH
Hylocichla mustelina

Size: 8" (20 cm)

Male: Reddish brown head, back and wings with color fading into a brown tail. A distinctive white breast, belly and sides, covered with black spots. White ring around black eyes, obvious on a black-streaked white face.

Female: same as male

Juvenile: similar to adult

Nest: cup; female builds; 1-2 broods per year

Eggs: 2-4; greenish blue without markings

Incubation: 13-14 days; female incubates

Fledging: 11-12 days; female and male feed young

Migration: complete, to Central and South America

Food: insects, fruit

Compare: Similar body shape as the American Robin (pg. 251), but lacks the Robin's red breast. Similar rusty color as the Brown Thrasher (pg. 153), but Brown Thrasher has a much longer rusty red tail and bright yellow eyes, compared with the shorter brown tail and black eyes of Wood Thrush.

Stan's Notes: One of the easier thrushes to identify due to the large dark spots on breast and belly. Well known for its liquid flute-like calls, heard deep within woodlots throughout Virginia. Returns to the same woodland each year during the last two weeks of March. Often is seen on the ground, hopping around like a robin in search of insects.

winter

breeding

SPOTTED SANDPIPER
Actitis macularia

Size: 8" (20 cm)

Male: Olive brown back. Long bill and long dull yellow legs. White chest. A white line over the eyes. Breeding adult has black spots on chest. Winter adult lacks breast spots.

Female: same as male

Juvenile: similar to winter adult, with a darker bill

Nest: ground; female and male build; 2 broods per year

Eggs: 3-4; brownish with brown markings

Incubation: 20-24 days; male incubates

Fledging: 17-21 days; male feeds young

Migration: complete, to southern coastal states, Mexico, Central and South America

Food: aquatic insects

Compare: Much smaller than the Greater Yellowlegs (pg. 165). Look for Spotted Sandpiper to bob its tail up and down while standing. Look for breeding Sandpiper's black spots extending from chest to abdomen.

Stan's Notes: One of the more common sandpipers. It is also one of the few shorebirds that will dive underwater if pursued. Able to fly straight up out of water. Flies with wings held in a cup-like arc, rarely lifting them above a horizontal plane. Constantly bobs its tail while standing and walks as if delicately balanced. Female mates with multiple males and lays eggs in up to five different nests. Male incubates and cares for young. In winter plumage, it lacks spots.

winter pg. 241

breeding

SANDERLING
Calidris alba

MIGRATION
WINTER

Size: 8" (20 cm)

Male: During breeding season (April to August), has a rusty-colored head, breast and back with a white belly. Black legs and bill.

Female: same as male

Juvenile: spotty black on head and back, with white belly, black legs and bill

Nest: ground; male builds; 1-2 broods per year

Eggs: 3-4; greenish olive with brown markings

Incubation: 24-30 days; male and female incubate

Fledging: 16-17 days; female and male feed young

Migration: partial migrator to complete, to West Indies and East, Gulf and South American coasts

Food: insects

Compare: Same size as the breeding plumage Spotted Sandpiper (pg. 133), but lacks chest spots.

Stan's Notes: One of the most common shorebirds in Virginia, but mostly seen in gray winter plumage from August to April. Can be seen in groups on sandy beaches, running out with each retreating wave to feed. Look for a flash of white on wings when it's in flight. Occasionally the female will mate with several males (polyandry), resulting in males and the female incubating separate nests. Both sexes will perform a distraction display if threatened. Nests on the Arctic tundra.

winter
pg. 243

breeding

DUNLIN
Calidris alpina

MIGRATION
WINTER

Size: 8-9" (20-22.5 cm)

Male: Distinctive breeding adult has a rusty red back, finely streaked chest and an obvious black patch on the belly. Stout bill, curving slightly downward at the tip. Black legs.

Female: slightly larger than male, with a longer bill

Juvenile: slightly rusty back with a spotty chest

Nest: ground; the male and female build; 1 brood per year

Eggs: 2-4; an olive-buff or a blue-green with red-brown markings

Incubation: 21-22 days; male and female incubate, the male during day, female at night

Fledging: 19-21 days; male feeds young, female often leaves before young fledge

Migration: complete, to the coasts of the U.S., Mexico and Central America

Food: insects

Compare: Similar in size to the breeding Sanderling (pg. 135), look for the obvious black belly patch and curved bill of breeding Dunlin.

Stan's Notes: Breeding plumage more commonly seen in spring. Flights include heights of up to 100 feet (30 m) with brief gliding alternating with shallow flutters, and a rhythmic, repeating song. Huge flocks fly synchronously, with birds twisting and turning, flashing light and dark undersides. Males tend to fly farther south in winter than females. A winter visitor along the coast, it doesn't nest in Virginia.

male pg. 293

female

NORTHERN CARDINAL
Cardinalis cardinalis

YEAR-ROUND

Size: 8-9" (20-22.5 cm)

Female: Buff brown bird with tinges of red on crest and wings, a black mask and large red bill.

Male: red bird with a black mask extending from face down to chin and throat, large red bill and crest

Juvenile: same as female, but with a blackish gray bill

Nest: cup; female builds; 2-3 broods per year

Eggs: 3-4; bluish white with brown markings

Incubation: 12-13 days; female and male incubate

Fledging: 9-10 days; female and male feed young

Migration: non-migrator

Food: seeds, insects, fruit; comes to seed feeders

Compare: Cedar Waxwing (pg. 127) has a small dark bill. Female Cardinal appears similar to the juvenile Cardinal. Look for female's bright red bill.

Stan's Notes: A familiar backyard bird. Look for the male feeding female during courtship. Male feeds young of the first brood by himself while female builds second nest. The name comes from the Latin word *cardinalis*, which means "important." Very territorial in spring, it will fight its own reflection in a window. Non-territorial during winter, gathering in small flocks of up to 20 birds. Both the female and male sing, and can be heard anytime of year. Listen for its "whata-cheer-cheer-cheer" territorial call in spring.

female

male pg. 9

RED-WINGED BLACKBIRD
Agelaius phoeniceus

YEAR-ROUND

Size: 8½" (22 cm)

Female: Heavily streaked brown bird with a pointed brown bill and white eyebrows.

Male: jet black bird with red and yellow patches on upper wings, pointed black bill

Juvenile: same as female

Nest: cup; female builds; 2-3 broods per year

Eggs: 3-4; bluish green with brown markings

Incubation: 10-12 days; female incubates

Fledging: 11-14 days; female and male feed young

Migration: non-migrator to partial migrator in Virginia

Food: seeds, insects; will come to seed feeders

Compare: Slightly larger than female Brown-headed Cowbird (pg. 129), which lacks the white eyebrows and streaks on breast. Similar to female Rose-breasted Grosbeak (pg. 123), but the Red-winged has a thinner body and pointed bill.

Stan's Notes: One of the most widespread and numerous birds in Virginia. It is a sure sign of spring when the Red-winged Blackbirds return to the marshes. Flocks of up to 100,000 birds have been reported. Males return before the females and defend territories by singing from tops of surrounding vegetation. Males repeat call from the tops of cattails while showing off their red and yellow wing bars (epaulets). Females choose mate and usually will nest over shallow water in thick stands of cattails. Red-wingeds feed mostly on seeds in fall and spring, switching to insects during summer.

in flight

COMMON NIGHTHAWK
Chordeiles minor

SUMMER

Size: 9" (22.5 cm)

Male: A camouflaged brown and white bird with white chin. A distinctive white band across wings and the tail, seen only in flight.

Female: similar to male, but with tan chin, lacks the white tail band

Juvenile: similar to female

Nest: no nest; lays eggs on the ground, usually on rocks, or on rooftop; 1 brood per year

Eggs: 2; cream with lavender markings

Incubation: 19-20 days; female and male incubate

Fledging: 20-21 days; female and male feed young

Migration: complete, to South America

Food: insects caught in air

Compare: Male Whip-poor-will (pg. 145) is similar in size, but much browner. Look for the white chin and wing band of Nighthawk in flight. Chimney Swift (pg. 91) is much smaller. Look for Nighthawk's characteristic flap-flap-flap-glide flight pattern.

Stan's Notes: Usually only seen flying at dusk or after sunset, but not uncommon for it to be sitting on a fence post, sleeping during the day. A very noisy bird, repeating a "peenting" call during flight. Alternates slow wing beats with bursts of quick wing beats. Prolific insect eater. Prefers gravel rooftops for nesting in cities and nests on the ground in country. Male's distinctive springtime mating ritual is a steep diving flight terminated with a loud popping noise. One of the first birds to migrate each fall, starting in August.

WHIP-POOR-WILL
Caprimulgus vociferus

SUMMER

Size: 10" (25 cm)

Male: Mottled brown and black. Distinctive black chin and a white U-shaped throat marking.

Female: same as male, but has a brown chin and tan throat marking

Juvenile: similar to adult of the same sex

Nest: no nest; lays eggs on ground; 1-2 broods per year

Eggs: 2; white with brown markings

Incubation: 19-20 days; female and male incubate

Fledging: 18-20 days; female and male feed young

Migration: complete, to Mexico, Central America and South America

Food: insects

Compare: Male Common Nighthawk (pg. 143) has a distinctive white band across wings (seen in flight), which the Whip-poor-will lacks. Nighthawk is commonly seen flying, while Whip-poor-will is rarely seen flying.

Stan's Notes: A very well-known bird in Virginia, although rarely seen. Its repetitive nocturnal "whip-poor-will" call, usually heard only in the spring, is loved by many and hated by others. Nothing can be done to stop the nocturnal calling despite how much sleep you are losing. Generally found in woodland, Whip-poor-wills sit parallel on a branch during the day. They don't build nests, but lay eggs on the ground, selecting sites along forest edges. The male will care for its young if the female starts a second brood.

NORTHERN BOBWHITE
Colinus virginianus

Size: 10" (25 cm)

Male: Short, stocky, mostly brown bird with short gray tail. A prominent white eye stripe and white chin. Reddish brown sides and belly, often with black lines and dots.

Female: similar to male, with buff brown eye stripe and chin

Juvenile: smaller and duller than adults

Nest: ground; the female and male build; 1 brood per year

Eggs: 12-15; white to creamy without markings

Incubation: 23-24 days; female and male incubate

Fledging: 6-7 days; female and male feed young

Migration: non-migrator

Food: insects, seeds, fruit; will come to ground feeders offering corn and millet

Compare: Ruffed Grouse (pg. 181) is much larger and has a feathered tuft on head and neck ruffs.

Stan's Notes: Prefers shrubs, orchards, hedgerows and pastures. Moves around in small flocks of 20 birds (often family members), called a covey. The covey often rests together during the night, in a tight circle with tails together and heads facing outward, to watch for predators. Males and females perform distraction displays when nests or young are threatened. Nest is a depression in the ground lined with grass. Often pulls nearby vegetation over nest to help conceal it. Male gives a rising whistle, "bob-white," heard mainly in spring and summer. Also gives a single "hoy" call year-round.

winter pg. 255

breeding

SHORT-BILLED DOWITCHER
Limnodromus griseus

MIGRATION
WINTER

Size: 11" (28 cm)

Male: Breeding plumage is an overall rusty brown with heavy black spots throughout. Has a small amount of white very low on belly. A long, straight black bill. Off-white eyebrow stripe. Legs and feet dull yellow to green.

Female: same as male

Juvenile: similar to winter adult

Nest: ground; the female and male build; 1 brood per year

Eggs: 3-4; olive green with dark markings

Incubation: 20-21 days; male and female incubate

Fledging: 25-27 days; male and female feed young

Migration: complete, to coastal Virginia and southern coastal states, Central America

Food: insects, snails, worms, leeches, seeds

Compare: Marbled Godwit (pg. 185) is larger and has a two-toned, upturned bill and gray legs. Smaller than the breeding Willet (pg. 169), which has shorter bill, and bold black and white wing linings, as seen in flight.

Stan's Notes: Mostly a winter resident, it is most abundant during spring and fall migrations. Found on the coast and inland on freshwater lakes and marshes. With a rapid probing action like a sewing machine, uses its long straight bill to probe deep into sand and mud for insects. Can be seen with the less common Long-billed Dowitcher (not shown), but it is hard to tell the two apart. Doesn't nest in Virginia.

149

KILLDEER
Charadrius vociferus

YEAR-ROUND

Size: 11" (28 cm)

Male: An upland shorebird with two black bands around the neck like a necklace. A brown back and white belly. Bright reddish orange rump, visible in flight.

Female: same as male

Juvenile: similar to adult, with only one neck band

Nest: ground; male builds; 2 broods per year

Eggs: 3-5; tan with brown markings

Incubation: 24-28 days; male and female incubate

Fledging: 25 days; male and female lead their young to food

Migration: complete, to southern states, Mexico and Central America, non-migrator in Virginia

Food: insects

Compare: Semipalmated Plover (pg. 119) is smaller, shares the brown back and white belly, but has only one black necklace.

Stan's Notes: The only shorebird with two black neck bands. It is known for its broken wing impression, which draws intruders away from nest. Once clear of the nest, the Killdeer takes flight. Nests are only a slight depression in a gravel area, often very difficult to see. Young look like yellow cotton balls on stilts when first hatched, but quickly molt to appear similar to parents. Able to follow parents and peck for insects soon after birth. Is technically classified as a shorebird, but doesn't live at the shore. Often found in vacant fields or along railroads. Has a very distinctive "kill-jer" call.

BROWN THRASHER
Toxostoma rufum

Size: 11" (28 cm)

Male: A rusty red bird with long tail and heavily streaked breast and belly. Two white wing bars. Long curved bill. Bright yellow eyes.

Female: same as male

Juvenile: same as adult, but eye color is grayish

Nest: cup; female and male build; 2 broods a year

Eggs: 4-5; pale blue with brown markings

Incubation: 11-14 days; female and male incubate

Fledging: 10-13 days; female and male feed young

Migration: complete, to southern states, non-migrator in eastern Virginia

Food: insects, fruit

Compare: Slightly larger in size and similar in shape to the American Robin (pg. 251) and Gray Catbird (pg. 245), but the Thrasher has a streaked breast and rusty color. The Wood Thrush (pg. 131) has a shorter brown tail and black eyes, compared with Thrasher's longer rusty red tail and yellow eyes.

Stan's Notes: A prodigious songster, often in thick shrubs where it sings deliberate musical phrases, repeating each twice. Male has the largest documented song repertoire of all North American birds, with over 1,100 song types. Often seen quickly flying or running in and out of dense shrubs. Noisy feeding due to habit of turning over leaves, small rocks and branches. Populations increase during winter months from the influx of northern birds. More abundant in the central Great Plains than anywhere else in North America.

male

female

YEAR-ROUND

Size: 10-12" (25-30 cm); up to 2-foot wingspan

Male: Rusty brown back and tail. A white breast with dark spots. Double black vertical lines on white face. Blue gray wings. Distinctive wide black band with a white edge on tip of rusty tail.

Female: similar to male, but slightly larger, has rusty brown wings and dark bands on tail

Juvenile: same as adult of the same sex

Nest: cavity; doesn't build a nest within; 1 brood per year

Eggs: 4-5; white with brown markings

Incubation: 29-31 days; male and female incubate

Fledging: 30-31 days; female and male feed young

Migration: non-migrator to partial migrator

Food: insects, small mammals and birds, reptiles

Compare: Similar to other falcons. Look for the two vertical black stripes on face of Kestrel. No other small bird of prey has rusty-colored back or tail.

Stan's Notes: Formerly called Sparrow Hawk due to its small size. Could be called Grasshopper Hawk because it eats many grasshoppers. Hovers near roads before diving for prey. Adapts quickly to a wooden nesting box. Has pointed swept-back wings, seen in flight. Perches nearly upright. Unusual raptor in that males and females have quite different markings. Watch for them to pump their tails up and down after landing on perches.

female

male

NORTHERN FLICKER
Colaptes auratus

Size: 12" (30 cm)

Male: Brown and black woodpecker with a large white rump patch visible only when flying. Black necklace above a speckled breast. Red spot on nape of neck and black mustache.

Female: same as male, but lacking a black mustache

Juvenile: same as adult of the same sex

Nest: cavity; female and male excavate; 1 brood per year

Eggs: 5-8; white without markings

Incubation: 11-14 days; female and male incubate

Fledging: 25-28 days; female and male feed young

Migration: non-migrator in Virginia

Food: insects, especially ants and beetles

Compare: Yellow-bellied Sapsucker (pg. 35) is smaller, with red chin and forehead. The male Red-bellied Woodpecker (pg. 41) has a red cap and a black-and-white zebra-striped back, and lacks a mustache. Flickers are the only brown-backed woodpeckers in Virginia.

Stan's Notes: Populations swell in winter with northern migrants. The only woodpecker to regularly feed on the ground, preferring ants and beetles. Produces an antacid saliva to neutralize the acidic defense of ants. Male usually selects nest site, taking up to 12 days to excavate. Some have had success attracting flickers to nest boxes stuffed with sawdust. In flight, flashes golden yellow under wings and tail, undulates deeply and gives a loud "wacka-wacka" call.

15

YELLOW-BILLED CUCKOO
Coccyzus americanus

Size: 12" (30 cm)

Male: Grayish brown head, back, wings and tail. Undertail distinctively patterned with bold black and white spots and lines. A white chin, chest and belly, and long downward-curved bill. Lower bill (mandible) is yellow.

Female: same as male

Juvenile: similar to adult, undertail lacks bold black and white pattern, bill lacks yellow

Nest: platform; the female and male build; 1-2 broods per year

Eggs: 2-6; light blue without markings

Incubation: 9-11 days; female and male incubate

Fledging: 7-9 days; female and male feed young

Migration: complete, to South America

Food: insects

Compare: The large-sized, curved bill and bold black and white undertail markings make this bird hard to confuse with others.

Stan's Notes: A common summer resident throughout the state. Found in a wide variety of habitats, but usually nests along forest edges. Often will place a flimsy stick nest in a densely covered tree fork. Unlike many other birds, the young do not hatch at the same time (asynchronously). There can be many days between the first and last to hatch. Very short egg-to-fledging time with some young leaving the nest (fledging) after only one week. The first to fledge are attended by the male, while the female cares for the rest in the nest. Declining in population in many states.

MOURNING DOVE
Zenaida macroura

Size: 12" (30 cm)

Male: Smooth fawn-colored dove with gray patch on the head. Iridescent pink, green around neck. A single black spot behind and below eyes. Black spots on wings and tail. Pointed wedge-shaped tail with white edges.

Female: similar to male, lacking iridescent pink and green neck feathers

Juvenile: spotted and streaked

Nest: platform; female and male build; 2 broods per year

Eggs: 2; white without markings

Incubation: 13-14 days; male and female incubate, the male during day, female at night

Fledging: 12-14 days; female and male feed young

Migration: non-migrator to partial migrator; will move around to find food

Food: seeds; will come to seed feeders

Compare: Smaller than Rock Dove (pg. 261), lacking its wide range of color combinations.

Stan's Notes: Name comes from its mournful cooing. It mates for life, roughly seven to ten years. A ground feeder, bobbing its head as it walks. One of the few birds to drink without lifting head, same as Rock Dove. Parents feed their young a regurgitated liquid called crop-milk for the first few days of life. Flimsy platform nest of twigs often falls apart in a storm. Wind rushing through wing feathers in flight creates a characteristic whistling sound.

PIED-BILLED GREBE
Podilymbus podiceps

Size: 13" (33 cm)

Male: Small brown water bird with a black chin and black ring around a thick, chicken-like ivory bill. Puffy white patch under the tail. Has an unmarked brown bill during winter (October to February).

Female: same as male

Juvenile: paler than adult, with white spots and gray chest, belly and bill

Nest: floating platform; female and male build; 1 brood per year

Eggs: 5-7; bluish white without markings

Incubation: 22-24 days; female and male incubate

Fledging: 22-24 days; female and male feed young

Migration: complete, to southern states, Mexico and Central America, non-migrator in Virginia

Food: crayfish, aquatic insects, fish

Compare: The smallest brown water bird that dives underwater for long periods of time.

Stan's Notes: A common resident bird. Often seen diving for food. It slowly sinks like a submarine if disturbed. Once called Hell-diver because of the length of time it can stay submerged. Can surface far away from where it went under. Builds platform nest on a floating mat in water. Particularly sensitive to pollution. Adapted well to life on water, with short wings, lobed toes and legs set close to the rear of body. While swimming is easy, it is very awkward on land. The name "Grebe" probably came from the Old English *krib*, meaning "crest," a reference to the Great Crested Grebe found in Europe.

GREATER YELLOWLEGS
Tringa melanoleuca

Size: 14" (36 cm)

Male: A tall bird with bulbous head and long thin bill, slightly turned up. Gray streaking on chest and white belly. Long yellow legs.

Female: same as male

Juvenile: same as adult

Nest: ground; female builds; 1 brood per year

Eggs: 3-4; off-white with brown markings

Incubation: 22-23 days; female and male incubate

Fledging: 18-20 days; male and female feed young

Migration: complete, coastal states from Virginia to California, Mexico and South America

Food: small fish, aquatic insects

Compare: Similar in size to breeding Willet (pg. 169), with a longer neck, smaller head and bright yellow legs. Greater Yellowlegs is overall a more brown bird than the breeding Willet.

Stan's Notes: A common shorebird that can be identified by the slightly upturned bill and long yellow legs. Often seen resting on one leg, its long legs carry it through deep water. Feeds by rushing forward through the water, plowing its bill or swinging it from side to side, catching small insects or fish. A skittish bird quick to give an alarm call, causing flocks to take flight. Quite often moves into the water prior to taking flight. Has a variety of "flight" notes that it gives when taking off. Nests on the ground near water on the northern tundra of Labrador and Newfoundland.

female

male pg. 17

YEAR-ROUND

BOAT-TAILED GRACKLE
Quiscalus major

Size: 14" (36 cm), female
16" (40 cm), male

Female: A golden brown chest and head with nearly black wings and tail, lacking iridescence.

Male: iridescent blue-black bird with a very long tail and bright yellow eyes

Juvenile: similar to female

Nest: cup; female builds; 2 broods per year

Eggs: 2-4; pale greenish blue, brown markings

Incubation: 13-15 days; female incubates

Fledging: 12-15 days; female feeds young

Migration: non-migrator; moves around to find food

Food: insects, berries, seeds, fish; visits feeders

Compare: Female Boat-tailed Grackle fairly distinctive and not confused with many other birds.

Stan's Notes: A noisy bird of coastal saltwater and inland marshes, giving several harsh, high-pitched calls and several squeaks. Eats a wide variety of foods from grains to fish. Sometimes seen picking insects off the backs of cattle. Will also visit bird feeders. Makes a cup nest with mud or cow dung and grass. Nests in small colonies. Most nesting occurs from April through May. Boat-taileds on the Atlantic coast have bright yellow eyes, while the Gulf coast birds have dark eyes.

breeding

winter pg. 263

displaying

WILLET
Catoptrophorus semipalmatus

Size: 15" (38 cm)

Male: Brown breeding plumage with a brown bill and legs. White belly. Distinctive black and white wing lining pattern, seen in flight or during display.

Female: same as male

Juvenile: similar to breeding adult, more tan in color

Nest: ground; female builds; 1 brood per year

Eggs: 3-5; olive green with dark markings

Incubation: 24-28 days; male and female incubate

Fledging: unknown days; female and male feed young

Migration: complete, to southern coastal states, coastal Central and South America, non-migrator along coastal Virginia

Food: aquatic insects

Compare: Slightly larger than the Greater Yellowlegs (pg. 165), which has yellow legs. Marbled Godwit (pg. 185) has two-toned, upturned bill. The breeding Short-billed Dowitcher (pg. 149) has yellow greenish legs.

Stan's Notes: Common year-round, but less abundant in summer. Northern birds pass through Virginia to Florida and South America. Appears a rich, warm brown during the breeding season and rather plain gray in winter, but always has a striking black and white wing pattern when seen in flight. Uses its black and white wing patches to display to mate. Named after the "pill-will-willet" call it gives on breeding ground. Gives a "kip-kip-kip" alarm call as it takes flight. Nests along the East coast, in some western states and Canada.

female

male

BLUE-WINGED TEAL
Anas discors

Size: 15-16" (38-40 cm)

Male: Small, plain-looking brown duck speckled with black. A gray head with a large white crescent-shaped mark at base of bill. Black tail with small white patch. Blue wing patch (speculum) usually only seen in flight.

Female: duller version of male, lacks facial crescent mark and white patch on tail, showing only slight white at base of bill

Juvenile: same as female

Nest: ground; female builds; 1 brood per year

Eggs: 8-11; creamy white

Incubation: 23-27 days; female incubates

Fledging: 35-44 days; female feeds young

Migration: complete, to coastal Virginia and southern states, Mexico and Central America

Food: aquatic plants, seeds, aquatic insects

Compare: Male Blue-winged has a distinct white face marking. The female is nearly half the size of female Mallard (pg. 203) and is similar to female Wood Duck (pg. 189), but lacks Wood Duck's eye-ring and crest.

Stan's Notes: A common duck found mostly along the coast. An early migrator in Virginia, most breeding birds leave before other, more northern ducks arrive in fall. Builds nest some distance from water. Female will perform distraction display to protect nest and young. Male leaves female near end of incubation. Planting crops and cultivating to pond edges have caused a decline in population.

female

male pg. 49

LESSER SCAUP
Aythya affinis

Size: 16-17" (40-43 cm)

Female: Overall brown duck with dull white patch at base of light gray bill. Yellow eyes.

Male: white and gray, the chest and head appear nearly black but head appears purple with green highlights in direct sun, yellow eyes

Juvenile: same as female

Nest: ground; female builds; 1 brood per year

Eggs: 8-14; olive buff without markings

Incubation: 22-28 days; female incubates

Fledging: 45-50 days; female teaches young to feed

Migration: complete, Virginia, southern states, Mexico, Central America, northern South America

Food: aquatic plants and insects

Compare: Similar size as the female Ring-necked Duck (pg. 179), but lacking the white ring around the bill. Look for the white patch at base of bill to help identify the female Lesser Scaup. Male Blue-winged Teal (pg. 171) is smaller, with crescent-shaped white mark near bill.

Stan's Notes: A common wintering duck in Virginia, completely submerging itself to feed on the bottom of lakes, unlike dabbling ducks which only tip forward to reach bottom. Often seen in large flocks on lakes, ponds and sewage lagoons during migration and winter. When seen in flight, note the bold white stripe under the wings. An interesting baby-sitting arrangement in which groups of young are tended by one to three adult females. Prefers fresh water, but can be seen along the coast. Doesn't breed in Virginia.

soaring

BROAD-WINGED HAWK
Buteo platypterus

Size: 14-19" (36-48 cm); up to 3-foot wingspan

Male: A hawk slightly smaller than the American Crow, the Broad-winged has a brown back and rusty red barring on the chest. Tail has two or three wide black-and-white bands. White under the wings with black "finger-tips," as seen in flight.

Female: same as male

Juvenile: tail bands narrower and more numerous, a brown-streaked chest and belly

Nest: platform; female and male build, but female finishes; 1 brood per year

Eggs: 2-3; off-white with brown markings

Incubation: 28-32 days; female incubates, male feeds female during incubation

Fledging: 34-35 days; female and male feed young

Migration: complete, to Central and South America

Food: small mammals, small birds, large insects, snakes, frogs

Compare: Similar in size to Cooper's Hawk (pg. 265), but with a wider, shorter tail. Larger than Sharp-shinned Hawk (pg. 259). Look for the alternating black-and-white tail bands.

Stan's Notes: A very common woodland hawk in Virginia. Can be seen in large groups (kettles) migrating early in fall. Spends most of its time hunting small birds, snakes and frogs in dense woods. Short round wings propel it through dense woodland. Will scream "call" repetitively when intruders are near the nest.

soaring

RED-SHOULDERED HAWK
Buteo lineatus

Size: 15-19" (38-48 cm); up to 3½-foot wingspan

Male: Reddish (cinnamon) head, shoulders, chest and belly. Wings and back are dark brown with white spots. Long tail with thin white bands and wide black bands. Obvious red wing linings, seen in flight.

Female: same as male

Juvenile: similar to adult, lacks the cinnamon color, has a white chest with dark spots

Nest: platform; female and male build; 1 brood per year

Eggs: 2-4; white with dark markings

Incubation: 27-29 days; female and male incubate

Fledging: 39-45 days; female and male feed young

Migration: non-migrator to partial migrator; winters in the U.S.

Food: reptiles, amphibians, large insects, birds

Compare: Sharp-shinned Hawk (pg. 259) is smaller and lacks Red-shouldered's reddish head and belly. The Red-tailed Hawk (pg. 191) is larger and has a white breast.

Stan's Notes: Common woodland hawk in Virginia. Prefers to hunt along edges of forests, spotting snakes, frogs, insects, an occasional small bird and other prey as it perches. Often seen flapping with an alternating gliding pattern. Very vocal hawk with a distinct scream. Mates when 2 to 3 years old. Stays in same territory for many years. Starts building nest in February. Young leave the nest by June.

male pg. 51

female

RING-NECKED DUCK
Aythya collaris

Size: 17" (43 cm)

Female: Mainly brown back with light brown sides, a gray face and dark brown crown. White eye-ring extends into a line behind eyes. A white ring around bill. Top of head peaked.

Male: black head, breast and back, sides are gray to nearly white, bold white ring around bill and a second ring at the base of bill, top of head peaked

Juvenile: similar to female

Nest: ground; female builds; 1 brood per year

Eggs: 8-10; olive gray to brown without markings

Incubation: 26-27 days; female incubates

Fledging: 49-56 days; female teaches young to feed

Migration: complete, to Virginia, southern states, West Indies, Mexico and Central America

Food: aquatic plants and insects

Compare: Female Lesser Scaup (pg. 173) is similar in size. Look for female Ring-necked's white ring around the bill.

Stan's Notes: A common wintering duck in Virginia. Usually seen in larger freshwater lakes rather than saltwater marshes. A diving duck, watch for it to dive underwater to forage for food. Takes to flight by springing up off water. Named "Ring-necked" because of the cinnamon-colored collar (nearly impossible to see in the field). Also known as Ring-billed Duck due to obvious white ring on bill.

RUFFED GROUSE
Bonasa umbellus

Size: 16-19" (40-48 cm)

Male: Brown chicken-like bird with long squared tail. Wide black band near tip of tail. Is able to fan tail like a turkey. Tuft of feathers on the head stands like a crown. Black ruffs on sides of neck.

Female: same as male

Juvenile: same as adult

Nest: ground; female builds; 1 brood per year

Eggs: 9-12; tan with light brown markings

Incubation: 23-24 days; female incubates

Fledging: 10-12 days; female leads young to food

Migration: non-migrator

Food: seeds, insects, fruit, leaf buds

Compare: Much larger than the Northern Bobwhite (pg. 147) and lacks Bobwhite's eye stripe. Look for feathered tuft on head and black neck ruffs.

Stan's Notes: A common bird of deep woods. Often seen in aspen or other trees, feeding on leaf buds. In the more northern climates, grows bristles on its feet during the winter to serve as snowshoes. When there is enough snow, it will dive into a snowbank to roost at night. In spring, male raises crest, fans tail feathers, and stands on logs and drums with wings to attract females. Drumming sound comes from cupped wings moving air, not pounding on chest or log. Female will perform distraction display to protect young. Two color morphs, red and gray, most apparent in the tail. Black ruffs around the neck gave rise to its common name.

male pg. 53

female

HOODED MERGANSER
Lophodytes cucullatus

Size: 16-19" (40-48 cm)

Female: Sleek brown and rust bird with a red head. Ragged "hair" on back of head. Long, thin brown bill.

Male: same size and shape as female, but black back and rust sides, crest "hood" raises to reveal large white patch, long black bill

Juvenile: similar to female

Nest: cavity; female lines old woodpecker hole; 1 brood per year

Eggs: 10-12; white without markings

Incubation: 32-33 days; female incubates

Fledging: 71 days; female feeds young

Migration: complete, to coastal states and Mexico

Food: small fish, aquatic insects

Compare: Very similar to, but smaller than, the female Red-breasted Merganser (pg. 199), which has a larger, lighter-colored bill. Larger than female Lesser Scaup (pg. 173), which has a dull white patch at base of bill.

Stan's Notes: A small diving bird of shallow-water ponds, sloughs, lakes and rivers. Rarely found away from wooded areas, where it nests in natural cavities or nest boxes. The female will "dump" eggs into other female Hooded Merganser nests, resulting in 20 to 25 eggs in some nests. Has been known to share a nesting cavity with a Wood Duck, sitting side by side. The male Hooded Merganser can voluntarily raise and lower its crest to show off the large white head patch. A winter visitor that doesn't nest in Virginia.

MARBLED GODWIT
Limosa fedoa

Size: 18" (45 cm)

Male: A tawny brown overall with a darker back. Long, two-toned and slightly upturned bill with black tip and pinkish base. Long gray legs. Cinnamon under wings, seen in flight.

Female: same as male

Juvenile: similar to adult

Nest: ground; the female and male build; 1 brood per year

Eggs: 3-5; olive green with dark markings

Incubation: 21-23 days; male and female incubate

Fledging: 20-21 days; female and male feed young

Migration: complete, to the East and Gulf coasts, and coastal Central America

Food: aquatic insects, snails, worms, leeches

Compare: Larger than the breeding Willet (pg. 169). Same size as Whimbrel (pg. 187), which has a down-curved bill, compared with the slightly upturned bill of the Godwit. Larger than the more common breeding Short-billed Dowitcher (pg. 149), which has a straight black bill.

Stan's Notes: A winter resident that is easily identified by its very long, two-toned, slightly upturned bill. Uses its bill to probe deep into sand and mud for insects. Usually feeds in mid-thigh water. In the winter, prefers saltwater beaches and mud flats up and down the East coast. Returns to Prairie Pothole regions of North Dakota and Canada for nesting. Nests in short grass prairie near wetlands.

WHIMBREL
Numenius phaeopus

Size: 18" (45 cm)

Male: Heavily streaked bird, light brown to gray. Long down-curved bill and multiple dark brown stripes on crown. Dark line through eyes. Legs light gray to blue.

Female: same as male

Juvenile: similar to adult

Nest: ground; the female and male build; 1 brood per year

Eggs: 3-4; olive green with dark markings

Incubation: 27-28 days; male and female incubate

Fledging: 35-42 days; female and male feed young

Migration: complete, to the coasts of the U.S., Mexico, Central and South America

Food: insects, snails, worms, leeches, berries

Compare: Larger than the breeding Willet (pg. 169). Same size as the Marbled Godwit (pg. 185), which has an upturned bill, compared with Whimbrel's down-curved bill. Larger than the more common Short-billed Dowitcher (pg. 149), which has a straight black bill.

Stan's Notes: Mostly a winter resident, easily identified by its very long down-curved bill and brown stripes on head. Uses its bill to probe deep into sand and mud for insects. Unlike other shorebirds, berries become an important food source in summer. Is very vocal, giving single note whistles. Returns to tundra of northern Alaska for nesting. Doesn't breed until age 3 and has long-term pair bond. Adults leave breeding grounds up to two weeks before the young.

187

male pg. 275

female

WOOD DUCK
Aix sponsa

YEAR-ROUND

Size: 17-20" (43-50 cm)

Female: A small brown dabbling duck. Bright white eye-ring and a not-so-obvious crest. A blue patch on wing is often hidden.

Male: highly ornamented with a green head and crest patterned with white and black, rusty chest, white belly and red eyes

Juvenile: same as female

Nest: cavity; female lines old woodpecker cavity; 1 brood per year

Eggs: 10-15; creamy white without markings

Incubation: 28-36 days; female incubates

Fledging: 56-68 days; female teaches young to feed

Migration: partial to non-migrator in Virginia

Food: aquatic insects, plants, seeds

Compare: Smaller than the female Mallard (pg. 203) and similar to the female Blue-winged Teal (pg. 171). Mallard and Teal lack the female Duck's bright white eye-ring and crest.

Stan's Notes: A common duck of quiet, shallow backwater ponds. Nests in old woodpecker holes or in nest boxes. Often seen flying deep in forest or perched high on tree branches. Female takes flight with loud squealing call and enters nest cavity from full flight. Will lay eggs in a neighboring female nest (egg dumping), resulting in some clutches in excess of 20 eggs. Young stay in nest cavity only 24 hours after hatching, then jump from up to 30 feet (9 m) to the ground or water to follow their mother, never returning to the nest.

soaring

RED-TAILED HAWK
Buteo jamaicensis

YEAR-ROUND

Size: 19-25" (48-63 cm); up to 4-foot wingspan

Male: Large hawk with amazing variety of colors from bird to bird, from chocolate brown to nearly all white. Often brown with a white breast and a distinctive brown belly band. Rust red tail usually only seen from above. Underside of wing is white with small dark patch on leading edge near shoulder.

Female: same as male, only slightly larger

Juvenile: similar to adults, lacking the red tail, has a speckled chest and light eyes

Nest: platform; male and female build; 1 brood per year

Eggs: 2-3; white, without markings or sometimes marked with brown

Incubation: 30-35 days; female and male incubate

Fledging: 45-46 days; male and female feed young

Migration: non-migrator to partial migrator

Food: mice, birds, snakes, insects, mammals

Compare: Red-shouldered Hawk (pg. 177) and Sharp-shinned Hawk (pg. 259) are much smaller.

Stan's Notes: A common hawk of open country and cities in the state, often seen perched on freeway light posts, fences and trees. Look for it circling above open fields and roadsides, searching for prey. Their large stick nests are commonly seen along roads in large trees. Nests are lined with finer material such as evergreen needles. Will return to the same nest site each year. Doesn't develop red tail until second year.

BARRED OWL
Strix varia

YEAR-ROUND

Size: 20-24" (50-60 cm); up to 3½-foot wingspan

Male: A chunky brown and gray owl with a large head and dark brown eyes. Dark horizontal barring on upper chest. Vertical streaks on lower chest and belly. Yellow bill and feet.

Female: same as male, only slightly larger

Juvenile: light gray with a black face

Nest: cavity; does not add any nesting material; 1 brood per year

Eggs: 2-3; white without markings

Incubation: 28-33 days; female incubates

Fledging: 42-44 days; female and male feed young

Migration: non-migrator

Food: mammals, birds, fish, reptiles, amphibians

Compare: Lacks the "horns" of the Great Horned Owl (pg. 195) and ear tufts of the tiny Eastern Screech-Owl (pg. 249). Eastern Screech-Owl is less than half the size of Barred Owl.

Stan's Notes: A very common owl that can often be seen hunting in daytime, perching and watching for mice, birds and other prey. One of the few owls to take fish out of a lake. Prefers dense deciduous woodland with sparse undergrowth. Can be attracted with a simple nest box with a large opening, attached to a tree. The young will stay with their parents for up to four months after fledging. Often sounds like a dog barking just before giving an eight-hoot call that sounds like, "Who-cooks-for-you? Who-cooks-for-you?" The Great Horned Owl sounds like, "Hoo-hoo-hoo-hoooo!"

GREAT HORNED OWL
Bubo virginianus

Size: 20-25" (50-63 cm); up to 3½-foot wingspan

Male: Robust brown "horned" owl. Bright yellow eyes and V-shaped white throat resembling a necklace. Horizontal barring on the chest.

Female: same as male, only slightly larger

Juvenile: similar to adults, lacking ear tufts

Nest: no nest; takes over the nests of crows, Great Blue Herons and hawks, or will use partial cavities, stumps or broken-off trees; 1 brood per year

Eggs: 2; white without markings

Incubation: 26-30 days; female incubates

Fledging: 30-35 days; male and female feed young

Migration: non-migrator

Food: mammals, birds (ducks), snakes, insects

Compare: Barred Owl (pg. 193) has dark eyes and no "horns." Over twice the size of the Eastern Screech-Owl (pg. 249).

Stan's Notes: The largest owl in Virginia and one of the earliest nesting birds in the state, laying eggs in January and February. Has excellent hearing; able to hear a mouse moving beneath a foot of snow. "Ears" are actually tufts of feathers (horns) and have nothing to do with hearing. Not able to turn head all the way around. Wing feathers are ragged on the end, resulting in a silent flight. Eyelids close from the top down, like humans. Fearless, it is one of the few animals that will kill skunks and porcupines. Because of this, it is sometimes called Flying Tiger.

GLOSSY IBIS
Plegadis falcinellus

Size: 23" (58 cm); up to 3-foot wingspan

Male: Chestnut brown head and neck. Iridescent green and blue wings and tail. Appears to be all dark brown from a distance. Very long, down-curved yellowish bill with blue facial skin near base. Long off-yellow legs.

Female: same as male

Juvenile: same as adult, but lacks iridescent coloring

Nest: platform; female and male build; 1 brood per year

Eggs: 2-4; light blue without markings

Incubation: 20-21 days; female and male incubate

Fledging: 28-32 days; female and male feed young

Migration: complete, to southern coastal states

Food: aquatic insects, crustaceans

Compare: One of two ibis species in Virginia, the long, down-curved bill helps identify them. The Glossy Ibis is brown and not confused with the White Ibis (pg. 311), which is all white.

Stan's Notes: Seems to be on the increase in Virginia. Prefers fresh water over salt water, with crayfish a big part of the diet. From a distance the bird appears dark brown or nearly black, but when seen up close or through binoculars its iridescent green and bluish purple colors are amazing. Its long down-curved bill helps identify it in flight. Often seen flying in groups of 30 or more. Nests in large colonies with other wading birds. Most leave Virginia in winter, but some stay.

male pg. 279

female

RED-BREASTED MERGANSER
Mergus serrator

Size: 23" (58 cm)

Female: Overall brown-to-gray duck with a shaggy reddish head and crest. Long orange bill.

Male: shaggy green head and crest, a prominent white collar, rusty breast, black and white body, long orange bill

Juvenile: similar to female

Nest: ground; female builds; 1 brood per year

Eggs: 5-10; olive green without markings

Incubation: 29-30 days; female incubates

Fledging: 55-65 days; female feeds young

Migration: complete, to coastal Virginia and southern coastal states, Central America

Food: fish, aquatic insects

Compare: Very similar to, but larger than, the female Hooded Merganser (pg. 183), which has a smaller, darker bill than the bill of female Red-breasted Merganser.

Stan's Notes: A winter resident of Virginia, commonly seen on the coast. Arrives in late October, leaves in April. A very fast flier, often seen flying low and fast across water. Needs a long take-off run to get airborne. Serrated bill helps it catch slippery fish. Doesn't breed before 2 years of age. Males abandon females just after eggs are laid. Females often share a nest. Nests in northern Canada and Alaska.

male pg. 267

female

NORTHERN HARRIER
Circus cyaneus

YEAR-ROUND
MIGRATION
WINTER

Size: 24" (60 cm); up to 3½-foot wingspan

Female: A slim, low-flying hawk. Dark brown back with brown-streaked breast and belly. Large white rump patch and narrow black bands across tail. Tips of wings black. Yellow eyes.

Male: silver gray with large white rump patch and white belly, faint narrow bands across tail, tips of wings black, yellow eyes

Juvenile: similar to female, with an orange breast

Nest: platform, often on ground; female and male build; 1 brood per year

Eggs: 4-8; bluish white without markings

Incubation: 31-32 days; female incubates

Fledging: 30-35 days; male and female feed young

Migration: complete, to southern states, Mexico and Central America; winters in eastern Virginia

Food: mice, snakes, insects, small birds

Compare: Slimmer than Red-tailed Hawk (pg. 191). Look for black bands on tail and a white rump patch.

Stan's Notes: One of the easiest hawks to identify. Harriers glide just above ground, following contours of the land while searching for prey. Holds its wings just above the horizontal position, tilting back and forth in the wind, similar to Turkey Vultures. Formerly called Marsh Hawk due to its habit of hunting over marshes. Feeds on the ground. Will perch on the ground to preen and rest. At any age, has a distinctive owl-like face disk.

male pg. 281

female

MALLARD
Anas platyrhynchos

YEAR-ROUND

Size: 27-28" (69-71 cm)

Female: All brown with orange and black bill. Small blue and white wing mark (speculum).

Male: large, bulbous green head, white necklace, rust brown or chestnut chest, combination of gray and white on sides, yellow bill, legs and feet

Juvenile: same as female, but with a yellow bill

Nest: ground; female builds; 1 brood per year

Eggs: 7-10; greenish to whitish, unmarked

Incubation: 26-30 days; female incubates

Fledging: 42-52 days; female leads young to food

Migration: complete, to southern states, non-migrator in Virginia

Food: seeds, plants, aquatic insects; will come to ground feeders offering corn

Compare: The female Blue-winged Teal (pg. 171) is nearly half the size of the female Mallard. The female Wood Duck (pg. 189) is also smaller and has a white eye-ring.

Stan's Notes: A familiar duck of lakes and ponds, it's considered a type of dabbling duck, tipping forward in shallow water to feed on aquatic plants on the bottom. The name "Mallard" comes from the Latin *masculus*, meaning "male," referring to the habit of males not taking part in raising ducklings. Both female and male have white tails and white underwings. Black central tail feathers of male curl upward. Will return to place of birth.

WILD TURKEY
Meleagris gallopavo

YEAR-ROUND

Size: 36-48" (90-120 cm)

Male: Large, plump brown and bronze bird with striking blue and red bare head. Fan tail and long, straight black beard in center of chest. Spurs on legs.

Female: thinner and less striking than male, usually lacking breast beard

Juvenile: same as adult of the same sex

Nest: ground; female builds; 1 brood per year

Eggs: 10-12; buff white with dull brown markings

Incubation: 27-28 days; female incubates

Fledging: 6-10 days; female leads young to food

Migration: non-migrator

Food: insects, seeds, fruit

Compare: This bird is quite distinctive and unlikely to be confused with others.

Stan's Notes: The largest game bird in Virginia, and the bird from which the domestic turkey was bred. Almost became our national bird, losing to the Bald Eagle by a single vote. Once eliminated from many eastern states due to market hunting and loss of habitat, they were reintroduced widely in the 1960s to 1980s. Now populations are stable. Strong fliers, they can approach 60 miles (97 km) per hour. Can fly straight up, then away. Eyesight is three times better than in humans. Hearing is also excellent; able to hear competing males up to a mile away. Males hold "harems" of up to 20 females. Males are known as toms, females are hens and young are called poults. At night, they roost in trees.

juvenile

breeding

chick-feeding adult

BROWN PELICAN
Pelecanus occidentalis

YEAR-ROUND
SUMMER

Size: 48" (120 cm); up to 9-foot wingspan

Male: Gray brown body, black belly, exceptionally long gray bill. Breeding adult has white or yellow head with dark chestnut hind neck. Adult that is feeding chicks (chick-feeding adult) has a speckled white head. A non-breeding adult has a white head and neck.

Female: similar to male

Juvenile: brown with white breast and belly, does not acquire adult plumage until third year

Nest: platform; female and male build; 1 brood per year

Eggs: 2-4; white without markings

Incubation: 28-30 days; female and male incubate

Fledging: 71-86 days; female and male feed young

Migration: complete to partial along coastal Virginia

Food: fish

Compare: An unmistakable bird in Virginia.

Stan's Notes: A coastal bird of Virginia and recently an endangered species. Having suffered from eggshell thinning during the 1970s due to DDT and other pesticides, it is now reestablishing along the East, West and Gulf coasts. Captures fish by diving headfirst into the ocean, opening its large bill and "netting" fish with its gular pouch. Frequently seen sitting on posts around marinas. Nests in large colonies. Doesn't breed before the age of 3, when it obtains its breeding plumage.

RUBY-CROWNED KINGLET
Regulus calendula

Size: 4" (10 cm)

Male: Small, teardrop-shaped green-to-gray bird. Two white wing bars. Hidden ruby-colored crown. White eye-ring.

Female: same as male, but lacking the ruby crown

Juvenile: same as female

Nest: pendulous; female builds; 1 brood per year

Eggs: 4-5; white with brown markings

Incubation: 11-12 days; female incubates

Fledging: 11-12 days; female and male feed young

Migration: complete, to southern states, Mexico and Central America

Food: insects, berries

Compare: The female American Goldfinch (pg. 319) is larger, but shares the same olive color and unmarked breast. Look for the white eye-ring of Ruby-crowned Kinglet.

Stan's Notes: One of the smaller birds in Virginia, it takes a quick eye to see the male's ruby crown. Most commonly seen during the spring and autumn migrations, look for it flitting around thick shrubs low to the ground. Builds an unusual pendulous (sac-like) nest, intricately woven and decorated on the outside with colored lichens and mosses stuck together with spider webs. The nest is suspended from a branch overlapped by leaves, usually hung high in a mature tree. The name "Kinglet" comes from the Anglo-Saxon word *cyning*, or "king," referring to the male's ruby crown, and the diminutive suffix "let," meaning "small."

RED-BREASTED NUTHATCH
Sitta canadensis

YEAR-ROUND
WINTER

Size: 4½" (11 cm)

Male: A small gray-backed bird with a black cap and a prominent eye line. A rust red breast and belly.

Female: gray cap, pale undersides

Juvenile: same as female

Nest: cavity; female builds; 1 brood per year

Eggs: 5-6; white with red brown markings

Incubation: 11-12 days; female incubates

Fledging: 14-20 days; female and male feed young

Migration: irruptive; moves around the state in search of food

Food: insects, seeds; visits seed and suet feeders

Compare: Smaller than the White-breasted Nuthatch (pg. 219), with a red chest instead of white.

Stan's Notes: The Red-breasted Nuthatch behaves like the White-breasted Nuthatch, climbing down tree trunks headfirst. Similar to chickadees, visits seed feeders, quickly grabbing a seed and flying off to crack it open. Will wedge a seed into a crevice and pound it open with several sharp blows. The name "Nuthatch" comes from the Middle English moniker *nuthak*, referring to the bird's habit of wedging a seed into a crevice and hacking it open. Look for it in mature conifers, where it often extracts seeds from cones. Doesn't excavate a cavity as a chickadee might; rather, it takes over an old woodpecker or chickadee cavity. A winter visitor in Virginia that is common in some years and scarce in others.

BROWN-HEADED NUTHATCH
Sitta pusilla

Size: 4½" (11 cm)

Male: Gray back. Brown cap bordered by a black line that extends through eyes. A dull white chin, breast and belly. Pale gray spot at the nape of neck, hard to see from a distance.

Female: same as male

Juvenile: same as adult

Nest: cavity; the female and male build; 1 brood per year

Eggs: 3-5; white with dark markings

Incubation: 12-14 days; female incubates

Fledging: 18-19 days; female and male feed young

Migration: non-migrator

Food: insects, seeds; comes to seed feeders

Compare: Carolina Chickadee (pg. 217) is similar in size, but has a black cap, compared with the brown cap of the Nuthatch.

Stan's Notes: A tiny bird of open pine forest in eastern Virginia. Like other nuthatches, it feeds by creeping up and down twigs and trunks of trees, looking for insects and insect eggs. Works hard to remove seeds from cones on evergreen trees. Has been known to cache pine seeds for later consumption. Will visit seed feeders. A cavity nester, it excavates a cavity, takes an abandoned woodpecker home or uses a nesting box. Occasionally an unmated male helper attends to a mated female on the nest. Will remain with mate nearly all year, defending a very small territory.

BLACK-CAPPED CHICKADEE
Poecile atricapilla

Size: 5" (13 cm)

Male: Familiar gray bird with black cap and throat patch. White chest. Tan belly. Small white wing marks.

Female: same as male

Juvenile: same as adult

Nest: cavity; female and male build or excavate; 1 brood per year

Eggs: 5-7; white with fine brown markings

Incubation: 11-13 days; female and male incubate

Fledging: 14-18 days; female and male feed young

Migration: non-migrator

Food: insects, seeds, fruit; comes to seed and suet feeders

Compare: Identical to Carolina Chickadee (pg. 217), except in song. Carolina's song is a higher, faster version of Black-capped Chickadee's. Tufted Titmouse (pg. 227) is larger than the Black-capped Chickadee and has a crest.

Stan's Notes: A backyard bird in western Virginia, attracted with a nest box or seed feeder. Usually the first to find a new feeder. Can be easily tamed and hand fed. Can be a common urban bird since much of its diet is from feeders. Needs to feed every day in winter; consequently seen foraging for food during even the worst winter storms. Often seen with nuthatches and woodpeckers. Makes its nest mostly with green moss, lining it with animal fur. Name comes from its "chika-dee-dee-dee-dee" call. Also gives a high-pitched, two-toned "fee-bee" call. Can have different calls in various regions.

215

CAROLINA CHICKADEE
Poecile carolinensis

Size: 5" (13 cm)

Male: Mostly gray bird with a black cap and chin. White face and chest with tan belly. Darker gray tail.

Female: same as male

Juvenile: same as adult

Nest: cavity; female and male build or excavate; 1-2 broods per year

Eggs: 5-7; white with reddish brown markings

Incubation: 11-12 days; female and male incubate

Fledging: 13-17 days; female and male feed young

Migration: non-migrator

Food: insects, seeds, fruit; comes to seed and suet feeders

Compare: Identical to the Black-capped Chickadee (pg. 215), except in song. Brown-headed Nuthatch (pg. 213) has a brown cap. The Tufted Titmouse (pg. 227) has an erect crest, and lacks the black cap and chin.

Stan's Notes: Widespread bird in Virginia and the most common chickadee in the state. One of the first birds to use a newly placed bird feeder. Flies to a feeder, grabs a single seed and carries it to a branch. To get to the meat inside, holds the seed down with its feet and hammers the shell open with bill. Returns for another seed. A friendly bird that can be tamed and hand fed. Can be attracted with a nest box with a 1¼-inch entrance hole. Female will give a loud snake-like hiss if disturbed on the nest. Often seen with other birds (mixed flock) in winter. A high, fast "chika-dee-dee-dee-dee" song.

YEAR-ROUND

WHITE-BREASTED NUTHATCH
Sitta carolinensis

Size: 5-6" (13-15 cm)

Male: Slate gray bird with a white belly, black cap and neck. Long thin bill, slightly upturned. Chestnut-colored undertail.

Female: similar to male, gray cap and neck

Juvenile: similar to female

Nest: cavity; the female and male build; 1 brood per year

Eggs: 5-7; white with brown markings

Incubation: 11-12 days; female incubates

Fledging: 13-14 days; female and male feed young

Migration: non-migrator

Food: insects, seeds; visits seed and suet feeders

Compare: Red-breasted Nuthatch (pg. 211) is smaller, with a rust red belly and a distinctive black eye line.

Stan's Notes: The nuthatch's habit of hopping headfirst down tree trunks helps it see insects and insect eggs that birds climbing up the trunk might miss. Incredible climbing agility comes from an extra-long hind toe claw or nail, nearly twice the size of the front toe claws. The name "Nuthatch" comes from the Middle English moniker *nuthak*, referring to the bird's habit of wedging a seed into a crevice and hacking it open. Frequently seen in mixed flocks of chickadees and Downy Woodpeckers. A year-round resident that is abundant throughout Virginia. Mated pairs stay together all year, defending small territories. Listen for its characteristic spring call, "whi-whi-whi-whi," given during February and March. One of 17 worldwide nuthatch species.

male

female

YELLOW-RUMPED WARBLER
Dendroica coronata

MIGRATION
WINTER

Size: 5-6" (13-15 cm)

Male: Slate gray bird with black mask and breast. Yellow patch on the head, flanks and rump. White chin and belly. Two white wing bars.

Female: similar to male, duller color, mostly brown and white with matching yellow patches

Juvenile: similar to female

Nest: cup; female builds; 2 broods per year

Eggs: 4-5; white with brown markings

Incubation: 12-13 days; female incubates

Fledging: 10-12 days; female and male feed young

Migration: complete, to southern states, Mexico and Central America; winters in Virginia

Food: insects, berries; rarely comes to suet feeders

Compare: Male Yellow Warbler (pg. 323) is all yellow with orange streaks on chest. Palm Warbler (pg. 327) has a yellow throat and chestnut crown. Common Yellowthroat (pg. 321) has a yellow breast. Look for a combination of yellow patches on the Yellow-rumped's head, flanks and rump.

Stan's Notes: One of the most common winter warblers, it is seen mostly from September to May. More common along the coast, less common in higher elevations. Male molts to a dull color in winter similar to female, retaining the yellow patches. Occasionally called Butter-butts due to the yellow patch on rump. Formerly known as Audubon's Warbler or Myrtle Warbler. Its familiar call is a robust "chip." Nests in coniferous and aspen forests.

YELLOW-THROATED WARBLER
Dendroica dominica

SUMMER

Size: 5½" (14 cm)

Male: A gray-backed warbler with a bright yellow throat. Black streaks on white belly. A white spot on neck and white eyebrows.

Female: same as male, but duller with browner back

Juvenile: similar to female

Nest: cup; the female and male build; 1-2 broods per year

Eggs: 4-5; gray with dark markings

Incubation: 12-13 days; female incubates

Fledging: 10-12 days; female and male feed young

Migration: complete, to Central and South America

Food: insects

Compare: Same size as the Yellow-rumped Warbler (pg. 221), which has yellow on head, flanks and rump, and lacks a yellow throat. Prairie Warbler (pg. 325) lacks Yellow-throated's gray back. Palm Warbler (pg. 327) has a chestnut cap.

Stan's Notes: One of the most widespread of Virginia's nesting warblers. Among the first returning warblers to the state, usually around mid-April. Prefers cypress and oak woodland. Finds food by creeping along and searching beneath vertical surfaces such as tree bark. Highly attracted to water, it is often seen bathing in any puddle of water. In some, the white eyebrows are tinged yellow. It is rarely a Brown-headed Cowbird host.

female
pg. 105

male

DARK-EYED JUNCO
Junco hyemalis

YEAR-ROUND
WINTER

Size: 5½" (14 cm)

Male: A round, dark-eyed bird with slate-gray-to-charcoal chest, head and back. White belly. Pink bill. Since the outermost tail feathers are white, tail appears as a white V in flight.

Female: same as male, only tan-to-brown color

Juvenile: similar to female, but has a streaked breast and head

Nest: cup, female and male build; 2 broods a year

Eggs: 3-5; white with reddish brown markings

Incubation: 12-13 days; female incubates

Fledging: 10-13 days; male and female feed young

Migration: complete, throughout the U.S.; winters in Virginia

Food: seeds, insects; will come to seed feeders

Compare: Rarely confused with any other bird. Large flocks feed under bird feeders in winter.

Stan's Notes: A common winter bird of Virginia. Usually seen on the ground in small flocks. Migrates from Canada to Virginia and beyond. Males tend to migrate farther south than females. Adheres to a rigid social hierarchy, with the dominant birds chasing the less dominant birds. Look for white outer tail feathers flashing while it's in flight. Most comfortable on the ground, juncos will use both feet to "double-scratch," exposing seeds and insects. Consumes many weed seeds. Several junco species have now been combined into one, simply called Dark-eyed Junco. Nests in western Virginia.

TUFTED TITMOUSE
Baeolophus bicolor

YEAR-ROUND

Size: 6" (15 cm)

Male: Slate gray bird with a white chest and belly. Pointed crest. Flanks are washed in a rusty brown. Gray legs and dark eyes.

Female: same as male

Juvenile: same as adult

Nest: cavity; female lines old woodpecker hole; 2 broods per year

Eggs: 5-7; white with brown markings

Incubation: 13-14 days; female incubates

Fledging: 15-18 days; female and male feed young

Migration: non-migrator

Food: insects, seeds, fruit; will come to seed and suet feeders

Compare: Closely related to the slightly smaller Black-capped Chickadee (pg. 215) and Carolina Chickadee (pg. 217), but Tufted Titmouse has a crest. Similar in size and color to the White-breasted Nuthatch (pg. 219), but Nuthatch lacks a crest.

Stan's Notes: A common feeder bird, it can be attracted with black oil sunflower seeds. Well known for its quickly repeated "peter-peter-peter" call. Prefix "Tit" comes from a Scandinavian word meaning "little." Suffix "mouse" is derived from the Old English word *mase*, meaning "bird." Simply translated, it is "a small bird." Notorious for pulling hair from sleeping dogs, cats and squirrels to line their nests. Attracted with nest boxes. Usually seen only one or two at a time. Male feeds female during courtship and nesting.

breeding
pg. 113

winter

MIGRATION
WINTER

Size: 6" (15 cm)

Male: Overall gray to light brown winter plumage with a distinct brown breast band and light gray eyebrows. White belly and dull yellow legs. Short, down-curved black bill.

Female: same as male

Juvenile: similar to winter adult, but buff brown and lacking the breast band

Nest: ground; the male and female build; 1 brood per year

Eggs: 3-4; olive with dark markings

Incubation: 19-23 days; male and female incubate

Fledging: 25-28 days; male and female feed young

Migration: complete, to coastal Virginia and southern coastal states, Central America

Food: insects, aquatic insects, seeds

Compare: The smallest of sandpipers. Often confused with winter Western Sandpiper (pg. 233) and Semipalmated Sandpiper (pg. 231), Least Sandpiper's yellow legs differentiate it from other tiny sandpipers. The short, thin, down-curved bill also helps to identify.

Stan's Notes: Seen during migration throughout Virginia. Winters in southern coastal states from Virginia to California. The smallest of peeps (sandpipers) that nest on the tundra in northern Canada and Alaska. Its yellow legs can be difficult to see in water, poor light or if covered with mud. Prefers the grassy flats of both saltwater and freshwater ponds. Can be approached without scaring.

229

breeding

winter

SEMIPALMATED SANDPIPER
Calidris pusilla

MIGRATION

Size: 6" (15 cm)

Male: Plump gray shorebird with black legs and a short, straight, blunt-tipped black bill. Has grayish brown head, neck and back, white breast and eyebrows in its winter plumage. Breeding (usually seen in the Arctic) has a brown head, some black and brown spots on the back, and a white belly.

Female: same as male

Juvenile: overall gray-brown with black spots

Nest: ground; the male and female build; 1 brood per year

Eggs: 2-4; light yellow with brown markings

Incubation: 18-22 days; male and female incubate

Fledging: 18-20 days; male and female feed young

Migration: complete, to Bahamas and northern South America

Food: aquatic insects

Compare: Much smaller and darker gray than winter Sanderling (pg. 241).

Stan's Notes: A common shorebird in Virginia. Seen during spring migration (mid-May to early June) and autumn migration (August to October). Few individuals stay year-round. Males do most of the care of young after hatching, since females abandon their families about two to three days after eggs hatch. Will retain same mate for several years. Nests in northern Canada and Alaska.

breeding
pg. 115

winter

WESTERN SANDPIPER
Calidris mauri

MIGRATION
WINTER

Size: 6½" (16 cm)

Male: Winter plumage is dull gray to light brown overall with a white belly and eyebrows. Black legs. Narrow bill that droops near tip.

Female: same as male

Juvenile: similar to breeding adult, bright buff brown on back only

Nest: ground; the male and female build; 1 brood per year

Eggs: 2-4; light brown with dark markings

Incubation: 20-22 days; male and female incubate

Fledging: 19-21 days; male and female feed young

Migration: complete, to coastal Virginia and southern coastal states, Central America

Food: insects, aquatic insects

Compare: Very often confused with the winter Least Sandpiper (pg. 229) and the Semipalmated Sandpiper (pg. 231). Look for black legs to differentiate from Least Sandpiper. Western has a longer bill that droops slightly at tip.

Stan's Notes: A winter resident in southern coastal states from Virginia to California. Nests on the ground in large "loose" colonies on the tundra of northern coastal Alaska. Adults leave breeding grounds several weeks before young. Some obtain their breeding plumage before leaving Virginia in spring. Feeds in deeper water than the Semipalmated Sandpiper.

233

EASTERN PHOEBE
Sayornis phoebe

YEAR-ROUND
SUMMER

Size: 7" (18 cm)

Male: Gray bird with dark wings, light olive green belly and a thin dark bill.

Female: same as male

Juvenile: same as adult

Nest: cup; female builds; 2 broods per year

Eggs: 4-5; white without markings

Incubation: 15-16 days; female incubates

Fledging: 15-16 days; male and female feed young

Migration: complete, to southern states and Mexico

Food: insects

Compare: Like most other olive gray birds, it is hard to distinguish identifying markings. Eastern Phoebe lacks any white eye-ring. Easier to identify by well-enunciated song, "fee-bee," or characteristic of hawking for insects.

Stan's Notes: A sparrow-sized bird often seen on the end of a dead branch. It sits in wait for a passing insect, flies out to catch it, then returns to the same branch, a process called hawking. Has a habit of pumping its tail up and down and spreading it when perched. Will build its nest under the eaves of a house, under a bridge or in culverts. Nest is constructed with mud, grass and moss, and lined with hair (and sometimes feathers). The name is derived from its characteristic song, "fee-bee," which is repeated over and over from the tops of dead branches.

GREAT CRESTED FLYCATCHER
Myiarchus crinitus

Size: 8" (20 cm)

Male: Gray head with prominent crest. Gray back and throat with bright yellow belly, yellow extending under reddish brown tail. Lower bill is yellow at base.

Female: same as male

Juvenile: same as adult

Nest: cavity; the female and male build; 1 brood per year

Eggs: 4-6; white or buff with brown markings

Incubation: 13-15 days; female incubates

Fledging: 14-21 days; female and male feed young

Migration: complete, to Mexico and Central America

Food: insects, fruit

Compare: The Eastern Kingbird (pg. 239) has a white band across the tail. Similar to the Eastern Phoebe (pg. 235), but the Flycatcher has an obvious crest and yellow belly.

Stan's Notes: Breeds throughout Virginia. Common in almost any wooded area, it lives high up in trees, rarely coming to the ground. Often heard before seen. The first part of its common name refers to the set of extra long feathers on the top of its head (crest), which the bird raises when alert or agitated, similar to Northern Cardinals. Feeds by gleaning insects from tree leaves. Nests in old woodpecker holes, but can be attracted to a nest box placed high in a tree with a 1½- to 2½-inch (4 to 6 cm) entrance hole. Often stuffs its nest with a collection of fur, feathers, string and snakeskins.

237

EASTERN KINGBIRD
Tyrannus tyrannus

SUMMER

Size: 8" (20 cm)

Male: Mostly black gray bird with white belly and chin. Black head and tail with a distinctive white band across the end of the tail. Has a concealed red crown that is rarely seen.

Female: same as male

Juvenile: same as adult

Nest: cup; male and female build; 1 brood a year

Eggs: 3-4; white with brown markings

Incubation: 16-18 days; female incubates

Fledging: 16-18 days; female and male feed young

Migration: complete, to Mexico, Central America and South America

Food: insects, fruit

Compare: Rarely confused with other birds. Medium-sized bird, smaller than American Robin (pg. 251). Look for the white band along the end of the tail to identify.

Stan's Notes: A common bird throughout Virginia in open fields and prairies. Autumn migration begins in late August and early September, with groups of up to 20 individuals migrating together. Returns to mating ground in spring, where male and female defend their territory. Acting unafraid of other birds and chasing the larger ones, it is perceived as having an attitude. Bold behavior gave rise to the common name, King. Perches on tall branches, watching for insects. After flying out to catch them, returns to the same perch, a technique called hawking.

breeding
pg. 135

winter

SANDERLING
Calidris alba

Size: 8" (20 cm)

Male: During winter, this is the lightest-colored sandpiper on the beach. Winter plumage head and back are gray and belly is white. Black legs and bill. White wing stripe, seen only in flight.

Female: same as male

Juvenile: spotty black on head and back, with white belly, black legs and bill

Nest: ground; male builds; 1-2 broods per year

Eggs: 3-4; greenish olive with brown markings

Incubation: 24-30 days; male and female incubate

Fledging: 16-17 days; female and male feed young

Migration: partial migrator to complete, to West Indies and East, Gulf and South American coasts

Food: insects

Compare: Same size as the winter plumage Spotted Sandpiper (pg. 133).

Stan's Notes: One of the most common shorebirds in Virginia, but mostly seen in gray winter plumage from August to April. Can be seen in groups on sandy beaches, running out with each retreating wave to feed. Look for a flash of white on wings when it's in flight. Occasionally the female will mate with several males (polyandry), resulting in males and the female incubating separate nests. Both sexes will perform a distraction display if threatened. Nests on the Arctic tundra.

winter

breeding
pg. 137

DUNLIN
Calidris alpina

Size: 8-9" (20-22.5 cm)

Male: Winter adult has a brownish gray back with a light gray chest and white belly. Stout bill curves slightly downward at tip. Black legs.

Female: slightly larger than male, with a longer bill

Juvenile: slightly rusty back with a spotty chest

Nest: ground; the male and female build; 1 brood per year

Eggs: 2-4; an olive-buff or a blue-green with red-brown markings

Incubation: 21-22 days; male and female incubate, the male during day, female at night

Fledging: 19-21 days; male feeds young, female often leaves before young fledge

Migration: complete, to the coasts of the U.S., Mexico and Central America

Food: insects

Compare: Similar size as winter Sanderling (pg. 241), but the winter Dunlin has a longer down-turned bill and is an overall darker gray.

Stan's Notes: Usually seen in gray winter plumage from August to early May. Breeding plumage is more commonly seen in the spring. Flights include heights of up to 100 feet (30 m) with brief gliding alternating with shallow flutters, and a rhythmic, repeating song. Huge flocks fly synchronously, with birds twisting and turning, flashing light and dark undersides. Males tend to fly farther south in winter than females. A winter visitor along the coast, it doesn't nest in Virginia.

243

GRAY CATBIRD
Dumetella carolinensis

YEAR-ROUND
SUMMER

Size: 9" (22.5 cm)

Male: Handsome slate gray bird with black crown and a long, thin black bill. Often seen with its tail lifted, exposing a chestnut-colored patch under tail.

Female: same as male

Juvenile: same as adult

Nest: cup; female and male build; 2 broods a year

Eggs: 4-6; blue green without markings

Incubation: 12-13 days; female incubates

Fledging: 10-11 days; female and male feed young

Migration: complete, to southern states, non-migrator in eastern Virginia

Food: insects, fruit

Compare: Larger than Eastern Phoebe (pg. 235), it lacks the Phoebe's olive belly. Similar size as Eastern Kingbird (pg. 239), but it lacks the Kingbird's white belly and white tail band.

Stan's Notes: Returns to the state by the last week of April. Seen in great numbers during fall migration in the last week of September and in early October. A secretive bird that the Chippewa Indians named Bird That Cries With Grief due to its raspy call. The call sounds like the mewing of a house cat, hence the common name. Often mimics other birds, rarely repeating the same phrases. More frequently heard than seen. Nests only in thick shrubs, and quickly flies back into shrubs if approached. If a cowbird introduces an egg into a catbird nest, the catbird will quickly break it, then eject it.

245

LOGGERHEAD SHRIKE
Lanius ludovicianus

YEAR-ROUND

Size: 9" (22.5 cm)

Male: A gray head and back with black wings and mask across the eyes. A white chin, breast and belly. Black tail, legs and feet. Black bill with hooked tip. White wing patches, seen in flight.

Female: same as male

Juvenile: dull version of adult

Nest: cup; the male and female build; 1-2 broods per year

Eggs: 4-7; off-white with dark markings

Incubation: 16-17 days; female incubates

Fledging: 17-21 days; female and male feed young

Migration: complete, to southern states and Mexico, non-migrator in Virginia

Food: insects, lizards, small mammals, frogs

Compare: The Northern Mockingbird (pg. 253) has a similar color pattern, but lacks the black mask of the Loggerhead. Shrike is stockier than the Mockingbird and perches in more open places.

Stan's Notes: The Loggerhead is a songbird that acts like a bird of prey. Known for skewering prey on barbed wire fences, thorns and other sharp objects to store or hold still while tearing apart to eat, hence its other name, Butcher Bird. Feet are too weak to hold prey while eating. During the winter, Loggerheads from northern states enter Virginia, increasing populations. On the decline overall due to pesticides killing its major food source–grasshoppers.

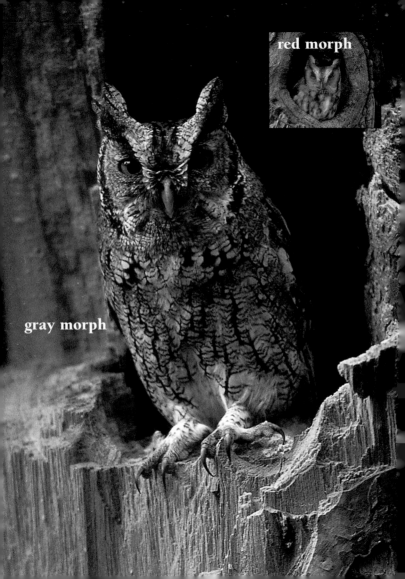

red morph

gray morph

EASTERN SCREECH-OWL
Otus asio

Size: 9" (22.5 cm); up to 20-inch wingspan

Male: Small "eared" owl that occurs in one of two permanent color morphs. Is either mottled with gray and white, or is red brown (rust) with white. Bright yellow eyes.

Female: same as male

Juvenile: lighter color than adult of the same morph, usually no ear tufts

Nest: cavity, former woodpecker cavity; does not add any nesting material; 1 brood per year

Eggs: 4-5; white without markings

Incubation: 25-26 days; female incubates, male feeds female during incubation

Fledging: 26-27 days; male and female feed young

Migration: non-migrator

Food: large insects, small mammals, birds, snakes

Compare: The only small owl in Virginia that has ear tufts. Can be gray or rust-colored.

Stan's Notes: A common owl active at dusk and during the night. Excellent hearing and eyesight. Will seldom give a screeching call; more commonly gives a tremulous, descending whiny trill, like a sound effect of a scary movie. Will nest in a wooden nest box. Often seen sunning themselves at nest box holes during the winter. Male and female may roost together at night, and are thought to mate for life. Different colorations are known as morphs. The gray morph is more common than the red.

AMERICAN ROBIN
Turdus migratorius

YEAR-ROUND

Size: 9-11" (22.5-28 cm)

Male: A familiar gray bird with a rusty red breast, and nearly black head and tail. White chin with black streaks. White eye-ring.

Female: similar to male, but with a gray head and a duller breast

Juvenile: similar to female, but has a speckled breast and brown back

Nest: cup; female builds with help from the male; 2-3 broods per year

Eggs: 1-7; pale blue without markings

Incubation: 12-14 days; female incubates

Fledging: 14-16 days; female and male feed young

Migration: complete, to southern states, Mexico and Central America, non-migrator in Virginia

Food: insects, fruit, berries, worms

Compare: Familiar bird to all.

Stan's Notes: Although complete migrators in northern states, the robin is a year-round resident in Virginia. Can be heard singing all night long in the spring. Most don't realize how easy it is to tell the difference between the male and female robins. Compare the male's dark, nearly black head and brick red breast with the female's gray head and dull red breast. Robins are not listening for worms when they cock their heads to one side. They are looking with eyes that are placed far back on the sides of their heads. A very territorial bird. Often seen fighting its own reflection in windows.

displaying

NORTHERN MOCKINGBIRD
Mimus polyglottos

Size: 10" (25 cm)

Male: Silvery gray head and back with light gray chest and belly. White wing patches, seen in flight or during display. Tail mostly black with white outer tail feathers. Black bill.

Female: same as male

Juvenile: dull gray overall, heavily streaked chest and gray bill

Nest: cup; female and male build; 2 broods per year, sometimes more

Eggs: 3-5; blue green with brown markings

Incubation: 12-13 days; female incubates

Fledging: 11-13 days; female and male feed young

Migration: non-migrator to partial migrator in Virginia

Food: insects, fruit

Compare: Loggerhead Shrike (pg. 247) has a similar color pattern, but is stockier, has a black mask and perches in more open places. Gray Catbird (pg. 245) is slate gray and lacks wing patches. Look for Mockingbird to spread its wings, flash its white wing patches and wag its tail from side to side.

Stan's Notes: Very animated, male and female perform elaborate mating dances by facing each other, heads and tails erect. They run toward each other, flashing white wing patches, and then retreat to nearby cover. Thought to also flash wing patches to scare up insects when hunting. Known to imitate other birds (vocal mimicry), hence its common name. Young males often sing at night.

breeding
pg. 149

winter

SHORT-BILLED DOWITCHER
Limnodromus griseus

MIGRATION
WINTER

Size: 11" (28 cm)

Male: Winter plumage back and wings are gray to light brown and the belly is white. Has a long, straight black bill. Off-white eyebrow stripe. Legs and feet dull yellow to green.

Female: same as male

Juvenile: similar to winter adult

Nest: ground; the female and male build; 1 brood per year

Eggs: 3-4; olive green with dark markings

Incubation: 20-21 days; male and female incubate

Fledging: 25-27 days; male and female feed young

Migration: complete, to coastal Virginia and southern coastal states, Central America

Food: insects, snails, worms, leeches, seeds

Compare: The winter Black-bellied Plover (pg. 257) is similar in size, but has a tiny bill, compared with Dowitcher's long bill. Smaller than the winter Willet (pg. 263), which has shorter bill, and bold black and white wing linings.

Stan's Notes: Mostly a winter resident, it is most abundant during spring and fall migrations. Found on the coast and inland on freshwater lakes and marshes. With a rapid probing action like a sewing machine, uses its long straight bill to probe deep into sand and mud for insects. Can be seen with the less common Long-billed Dowitcher (not shown), but it is hard to tell the two apart. Doesn't nest in Virginia.

breeding
pg. 45

winter

BLACK-BELLIED PLOVER
Pluvialis squatarola

MIGRATION WINTER

Size: 11-12" (28-30 cm)

Male: Winter plumage is uniform light gray with dark, nearly black streaks. White chest and belly. Faint white eyebrow mark. Black legs and bill.

Female: less black on chest and belly than male

Juvenile: grayer than adults, with much less black

Nest: ground; the male and female build; 1 brood per year

Eggs: 3-4; pinkish or greenish with black-brown markings

Incubation: 26-27 days; male and female incubate, the male during day, female at night

Fledging: 35-45 days; male feeds young, young learn quickly to feed themselves

Migration: complete, to the East and Gulf coasts, West Indies and coastal South America

Food: insects

Compare: Slightly larger than winter Dunlin (pg. 243) and lacking its long downward-curved bill.

Stan's Notes: The males perform a "butterfly" courtship flight to attract females. Female leaves male and young about 12 days after the eggs hatch. Breeds at 3 years of age. A common winter resident, arrivals start in July and August (autumn migration), and leaves in April. Doesn't breed in Virginia. In flight, in any plumage, displays a white rump and stripe on wings with black axillaries (armpits). Often darts across ground to grab an insect and run.

soaring

juvenile

SHARP-SHINNED HAWK
Accipiter striatus

YEAR-ROUND
WINTER

Size: 10-14" (25-36 cm); up to 2-foot wingspan

Male: Small woodland hawk with gray back and head, and rusty red breast. Long tail with several dark tail bands, widest band at end of squared-off tail. Red eyes.

Female: same as male, only larger

Juvenile: same size as adults, with a brown back and heavily streaked breast, yellow eyes

Nest: platform; female builds; 1 brood per year

Eggs: 4-5; white with brown markings

Incubation: 32-35 days; female incubates

Fledging: 24-27 days; female and male feed young

Migration: complete, to southern states, Mexico and Central America; winters in Virginia

Food: birds, small mammals

Compare: Nearly identical to Cooper's Hawk (pg. 265), only smaller. Look for the Sharp-shinned's squared tail, compared with the rounded tail of the Cooper's. Red-shouldered Hawk (pg. 177) is larger and lacks a gray back.

Stan's Notes: Common hawk of backyards and woodlands, often seen swooping in on birds visiting feeders. Short rounded wings and long tail allow this hawk to navigate through thick stands of trees in pursuit of prey. Common name comes from the sharp keel on the leading edge of its "shin," although it's actually below rather than above the bird's ankle on the tarsus bone of foot. The tarsus in most birds is round. In flight, head doesn't protrude as far as the head of the Cooper's Hawk.

ROCK DOVE
Columba livia

YEAR-ROUND

Size: 13" (33 cm)

Male: No set color pattern. Gray to white, patches of iridescent greens and blues, usually with a light rump patch.

Female: same as male

Juvenile: same as adult

Nest: platform; female builds; 3-4 broods a year

Eggs: 1-2; white without markings

Incubation: 18-20 days; female and male incubate

Fledging: 25-26 days, female and male feed young

Migration: non-migrator

Food: seeds

Compare: The Mourning Dove (pg. 161) is smaller and light brown in color.

Stan's Notes: Also known as Domestic Pigeon, it was introduced to North America from Europe by the early settlers. Most common around cities and barnyards, where it scratches for seeds. The wide color variation comes from the years of selective breeding while in captivity. Parents feed their young a regurgitated liquid known as crop-milk for the first few days of life. One of the few birds that can drink without tilting head back. Nests under bridges, on buildings, balconies, barns and sheds. Once poisoned as a "nuisance city bird," many cities have Peregrine Falcons (not shown) that feed on Rock Doves, keeping their numbers in check.

breeding
pg. 169

displaying

winter

WILLET
Catoptrophorus semipalmatus

YEAR-ROUND
MIGRATION

Size: 15" (38 cm)

Male: Winter plumage is gray with a gray bill and legs. White belly. A distinctive black and white wing lining pattern, seen in flight or during display.

Female: same as male

Juvenile: similar to breeding adult, more tan in color

Nest: ground; female builds; 1 brood per year

Eggs: 3-5; olive green with dark markings

Incubation: 24-28 days; male and female incubate

Fledging: unknown days; female and male feed young

Migration: complete, to southern coastal states, coastal Central and South America, non-migrator along coastal Virginia

Food: aquatic insects

Compare: Very similar to the light gray winter Short-billed Dowitcher (pg. 255), which has a longer bill, yellow greenish legs and rarely looks up from its constant feeding. Slightly larger than Greater Yellowlegs (pg. 165), which has yellow legs.

Stan's Notes: Common year-round, but less abundant in summer. Northern birds pass through Virginia to Florida and South America. In any plumage, always has a striking black and white wing pattern when seen during flight. Uses its black and white wing patches to display to mate. Named after the "pill-will-willet" call it gives while on the breeding ground. Gives a "kip-kip-kip" alarm call as it takes flight. Nests on the East coast, in some western states and Canada.

soaring

juvenile

COOPER'S HAWK
Accipiter cooperii

Size: 14-20" (36-50 cm); up to 2½-foot wingspan

Male: Medium-sized hawk with short wings and long rounded tail with several black bands. Rusty breast and dark wing tips. Slate gray back. Bright yellow spot at base of gray bill (cere). Dark red eyes.

Female: similar to male, only slightly larger

Juvenile: brown back with brown streaks on breast, bright yellow eyes

Nest: platform; male and female build; 1 brood per year

Eggs: 2-4; greenish with brown markings

Incubation: 32-36 days; female and male incubate

Fledging: 28-32 days; male and female feed young

Migration: non-migrator in Virginia

Food: small birds, mammals

Compare: Nearly identical to the Sharp-shinned Hawk (pg. 259), only larger, darker gray and with a rounded-off tail.

Stan's Notes: A common year-round resident hawk of woodland. In flight, look for its large head, short wings and long tail. The short stubby wings help it maneuver between trees while pursuing small birds. Will come to feeders, hunting for unaware birds. Flies with long glides followed by a few quick flaps. Known to ambush prey, it will fly into heavy brush or even run on the ground in pursuit. Nestlings have gray eyes that become bright yellow at 1 year of age and dark red later.

male

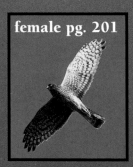

female pg. 201

NORTHERN HARRIER
Circus cyaneus

Size: 24" (60 cm); up to 3½-foot wingspan

Male: A slim, low-flying hawk. Silver gray with a large white rump patch and a white belly. Faint narrow bands across the tail. Tips of wings black. Yellow eyes.

Female: dark brown back, a brown-streaked breast and belly, large white rump patch, narrow black bands across tail, tips of wings black, yellow eyes

Juvenile: similar to female, with an orange breast

Nest: platform, often on ground; female and male build; 1 brood per year

Eggs: 4-8; bluish white without markings

Incubation: 31-32 days; female incubates

Fledging: 30-35 days; male and female feed young

Migration: complete, to southern states, Mexico and Central America; winters in eastern Virginia

Food: mice, snakes, insects, small birds

Compare: Slimmer than Red-tailed Hawk (pg. 191). Look for black bands on tail and a white rump patch.

Stan's Notes: One of the easiest hawks to identify. Harriers glide just above ground, following contours of the land while searching for prey. Holds its wings just above the horizontal position, tilting back and forth in the wind, similar to Turkey Vultures. Formerly called Marsh Hawk due to its habit of hunting over marshes. Feeds on the ground. Will perch on the ground to preen and rest. At any age, has a distinctive owl-like face disk.

CANADA GOOSE
Branta canadensis

YEAR-ROUND

Size: 25-43" (63-109 cm)

Male: Large gray goose with black neck and head, with a white chin or cheek strap.

Female: same as male

Juvenile: same as adult

Nest: platform, on the ground; female builds; 1 brood per year

Eggs: 5-10; white without markings

Incubation: 25-30 days; female incubates

Fledging: 42-55 days; male and female teach young to feed

Migration: non-migrator

Food: aquatic plants, insects, seeds

Compare: Large goose that is rarely confused with any other bird.

Stan's Notes: Formerly killed off (extirpated) in many areas, it was reintroduced and is now a common year-round resident. Adapting to our changed environment very well, it now breeds in Virginia. Adults mate for many years, but only start to breed in their third year. Males often act as sentinels, standing at the edge of the group, bobbing their heads up and down, becoming very aggressive to anybody approaching. Will hiss as if displaying displeasure. Adults molt primary flight feathers while raising their young, rendering family groups flightless at the same time. Several subspecies vary geographically around the U.S. Generally they are paler in color in eastern groups, darker in western. Size decreases northward, with the smallest subspecies found on the Arctic tundra.

GREAT BLUE HERON
Ardea herodias

YEAR-ROUND

Size: 42-52" (107-132 cm)

Male: Tall gray heron. Black eyebrows extend into several long plumes off the back of head. Long yellow bill. Feathers at base of neck drop down in a kind of necklace.

Female: same as male

Juvenile: same as adult, but more brown than gray, with a black crown and no plumes

Nest: platform; male and female build; 1 brood per year

Eggs: 3-5; blue green without markings

Incubation: 27-28 days; female and male incubate

Fledging: 56-60 days; male and female feed young

Migration: complete, to southern states, Mexico, and Central and South America, non-migrator in Virginia

Food: small fish, frogs, insects, snakes

Compare: Tricolored Heron (pg. 89) is half the size and has a white belly.

Stan's Notes: One of the most common herons, often barking like a dog when startled. Seen stalking small fish in shallow water. Will strike at mice, squirrels and just about anything else it might come across. Flies holding neck in an S shape, with its long legs trailing straight out behind. The wings are held in cupped fashion during flight. Nests in colonies of up to 100 birds. Nests in treetops near or over open water.

male

female

RUBY-THROATED HUMMINGBIRD
Archilochus colubris

Size: 3-3½" (7.5-9 cm)

Male: Tiny iridescent green bird with black throat patch that reflects bright ruby red in sun.

Female: same as male, but lacking the throat patch

Juvenile: same as female

Nest: cup; female builds; 1-2 broods per year

Eggs: 2; white without markings

Incubation: 12-14 days; female incubates

Fledging: 14-18 days; female feeds young

Migration: complete, to southern states, Mexico and Central America

Food: nectar, insects

Compare: No other bird is as tiny. The Sphinx Moth hovers at flowers like the Hummingbird, but has clear wings and a mouth part that looks like a straw, which coils up when not at a flower. Moves much slower than the Hummingbird and can be approached.

Stan's Notes: The smallest bird in Virginia. Able to hover, fly up and down, and is the only bird to fly backward. Does not sing, but will chatter or buzz to communicate. The wings create a humming noise, flapping 50 to 60 times per second or faster during chasing flights. Weighing just 2 to 3 grams, it takes about five average-sized hummingbirds to equal the weight of a single chickadee. Its heart pumps an incredible 1,260 beats per minute, and it breathes 250 times per minute. Constructs a nest with plant material and spider webs, gluing pieces of lichen on the outside of nest for camouflage. Attracted to tubular red flowers.

male

female pg. 189

WOOD DUCK
Aix sponsa

Size: 17-20" (43-50 cm)

Male: A small, highly ornamented dabbling duck with a green head and crest patterned with white and black. A rusty chest, white belly and red eyes.

Female: brown, similar size and shape as male, has bright white eye-ring and a not-so-obvious crest, blue patch on wing often hidden

Juvenile: same as female

Nest: cavity; female lines old woodpecker cavity; 1 brood per year

Eggs: 10-15; creamy white without markings

Incubation: 28-36 days; female incubates

Fledging: 56-68 days; female teaches young to feed

Migration: partial to non-migrator in Virginia

Food: aquatic insects, plants, seeds

Compare: Similar size as the male Hooded Merganser (pg. 53), which has a crest "hood" that it raises, revealing a large white patch.

Stan's Notes: A common duck of quiet, shallow backwater ponds. Nearly extinct around 1900 due to overhunting, but is doing well now. Nests in an old woodpecker hole or uses a nesting box. Often seen flying deep in forest or perched high on tree branches. Female takes flight with loud squealing call and enters nest cavity from full flight. Will lay eggs in a neighboring nest (egg dumping), resulting in some clutches in excess of 20 eggs. Young remain in nest cavity 24 hours after hatching, then jump from up to 30 feet (9 m) to the ground or water to follow their mother, never returning to the nest.

GREEN HERON
Butorides virescens

Size: 16-22" (40-56 cm)

Male: Short stocky heron with a blue-green back, and rusty red neck and chest. Dark green crest. Short legs, normally yellow, but turn bright orange during breeding season.

Female: same as male

Juvenile: similar to adult, with a blue-gray back and white-streaked chest and neck

Nest: platform; female and male build; 2 broods per year

Eggs: 2-4; light green without markings

Incubation: 21-25 days; female and male incubate

Fledging: 35-36 days; female and male feed young

Migration: complete, to South America, some move to Mexico and Central America

Food: fish, insects, aquatic plants

Compare: Green Heron is smaller than the Tricolored Heron (pg. 89) and lacks the long neck of most other herons. Look for a small heron with a dark green back stalking wetlands.

Stan's Notes: Often gives an explosive, rasping "skyew" call when startled. Sometimes it looks like it doesn't have a neck, because it holds its head close to its body. Hunts for fish and aquatic insects by waiting along a shore or wades stealthily. Has been known to place an object, such as an insect, on the water surface to attract fish to catch. Has a crest that it raises when excited. While most migrate each autumn, some will stay all winter along the coast.

female pg. 199

male

RED-BREASTED MERGANSER
Mergus serrator

MIGRATION
WINTER

Size: 23" (58 cm)

Male: A shaggy green head and crest. Prominent white collar. Rusty breast. Black and white body. Long orange bill.

Female: overall brown to gray with a shaggy reddish head and crest, long orange bill

Juvenile: similar to female

Nest: ground; female builds; 1 brood per year

Eggs: 5-10; olive green without markings

Incubation: 29-30 days; female incubates

Fledging: 55-65 days; female feeds young

Migration: complete, to coastal Virginia and southern coastal states, Central America

Food: fish, aquatic insects

Compare: Larger than the male Hooded Merganser (pg. 53), which has a large white patch on the head, compared with the green head of the male Red-breasted Merganser.

Stan's Notes: A winter resident of Virginia, commonly seen on the coast. Arrives in late October, leaves in April. A very fast flier, often seen flying low and fast across water. Needs a long take-off run to get airborne. Serrated bill helps it catch slippery fish. Doesn't breed before 2 years of age. Males abandon females just after eggs are laid. Females often share a nest. Nests in northern Canada and Alaska.

female pg. 203

male

MALLARD
Anas platyrhynchos

Size: 27-28" (69-71 cm)

Male: Large, bulbous green head, white necklace and rust brown or chestnut-colored chest. A combination of gray and white on sides. Yellow bill, legs and feet.

Female: all brown with orange and black bill, small blue and white wing mark (speculum)

Juvenile: same as female, but with a yellow bill

Nest: ground; female builds; 1 brood per year

Eggs: 7-10; greenish to whitish, unmarked

Incubation: 26-30 days; female incubates

Fledging: 42-52 days; female leads young to food

Migration: complete, to southern states, non-migrator in Virginia

Food: seeds, plants, aquatic insects; will come to ground feeders offering corn

Compare: Most people recognize this common duck. Larger than male Red-breasted Merganser (pg. 279), lacking the Merganser's shaggy crest and large orange bill.

Stan's Notes: A familiar duck of lakes and ponds, it's considered a type of dabbling duck, tipping forward in shallow water to feed on aquatic plants on the bottom. The name "Mallard" comes from the Latin *masculus*, meaning "male," referring to the habit of males not taking part in raising ducklings. Black central tail feathers of male curl upward. Both the male and female have white tails and white underwings. Will return to place of birth.

male

female pg. 331

BALTIMORE ORIOLE
Icterus galbula

MIGRATION
SUMMER

Size: 7-8" (18-20 cm)

Male: Bright flaming orange bird with black head and black extending down nape of neck onto the back. Black wings with white and orange wing bars. An orange tail with black streaks. Gray bill and dark eyes.

Female: pale yellow with orange tones, gray brown wings, white wing bars, gray bill, dark eyes

Juvenile: same as female

Nest: pendulous; female builds; 1 brood per year

Eggs: 4-5; bluish with brown markings

Incubation: 12-14 days; female incubates

Fledging: 12-14 days; female and male feed young

Migration: complete, to Mexico, Central America and South America

Food: insects, fruit, nectar; comes to orange half and nectar feeders

Compare: The male Orchard Oriole (pg. 285) is much darker orange than the Baltimore's brighter flaming orange color.

Stan's Notes: A fantastic songster, often heard before seen. Easily attracted to a feeder offering grape jelly, orange halves or sugar water (nectar). Parents bring young to feeders. Sits in tops of trees feeding on caterpillars. Female builds a sock-like nest at outermost branches of tall trees. Often returns to the same area year after year. Some of the last birds to arrive in spring (March to April) and first to leave in fall (August). Breeds throughout Virginia.

female pg. 333

male

ORCHARD ORIOLE
Icterus spurius

Size: 7-8" (18-20 cm)

Male: Dull orange bird with black head and black extending down the back. A black chin, tail and wings. Single white wing bars. A long, thin black bill with a small gray mark on lower mandible (jaw).

Female: olive green back with dull yellow belly, two white wing bars on dark gray wings

Juvenile: same as female, black bib on first-year male

Nest: pendulous; female builds; 1 brood per year

Eggs: 3-5; pale blue to white, brown markings

Incubation: 11-12 days; female and male incubate

Fledging: 11-14 days; female and male feed young

Migration: complete, central Mexico, Central America and northern South America

Food: insects, fruit; comes to fruit/nectar feeders

Compare: Similar to male Baltimore Oriole (pg. 283), but the male Orchard Oriole has a much darker orange body.

Stan's Notes: Prefers orchards or open woods, hence its common name. Eats insects until wild fruit starts to ripen. One of the last birds to arrive in spring and one of the first to leave in fall. Spends only four to five months in Virginia. Often migrates with the more abundant Baltimore Oriole. Usually will nest alone, but sometimes nests in small colonies. Parents bring the young to jelly and orange half feeders shortly after fledging. Many people mistakenly think the orioles have left during the summer but, in fact, these birds are concentrating on finding insects to feed their young.

yellow male

female pg. 97

male

HOUSE FINCH
Carpodacus mexicanus

YEAR-ROUND

Size: 5" (13 cm)

Male: An orange red face, breast and rump, with a brown cap. Brown marking behind eyes. Brown wings streaked with white. A white belly with brown streaks.

Female: brown with a heavily streaked white chest

Juvenile: similar to female

Nest: cup, sometimes in cavities; female builds; 2 broods per year

Eggs: 4-5; pale blue, lightly marked

Incubation: 12-14 days; female incubates

Fledging: 15-19 days; female and male feed young

Migration: non-migrator to partial migrator; will move around to find food

Food: seeds, fruit, leaf buds; will visit seed feeders

Compare: Male Purple Finch (pg. 289) is very similar, but male House Finch lacks the red crown. Look for the streaked breast and belly, and brown cap of male House Finch.

Stan's Notes: Very social bird. Visits feeders in small flocks. Likes nesting in hanging flower baskets. Incubating female is fed by the male. Has a loud, cheerful warbling song. House Finches originally introduced to Long Island, New York, from the western U.S. in the 1940s have since populated the entire eastern U.S. Now found all over the country. Suffers from a fatal eye disease that causes eyes to crust over. Rarely, some males are yellow (see inset) instead of red, probably due to poor diet.

female pg. 111

male

PURPLE FINCH
Carpodacus purpureus

Size: 6" (15 cm)

Male: Raspberry red head, cap, breast, back and rump. Brownish wings and tail.

Female: heavily streaked brown and white bird with large white eyebrows

Juvenile: same as female

Nest: cup; female and male build; 1 brood a year

Eggs: 4-5; greenish blue with brown markings

Incubation: 12-13 days; female incubates

Fledging: 13-14 days; female and male feed young

Migration: irruptive; moves around in search of food

Food: seeds, insects, fruit; comes to seed feeders

Compare: Redder than the orange red of male House Finch (pg. 287), with a clear (no streaking) red breast. The male House Finch has a brown cap, compared with the male Purple Finch's red cap.

Stan's Notes: Usually only seen in the winter, when Purple Finches leave their northern homes and move around, searching for food. Travels in flocks of up to 50. It is common in non-residential areas (prefers open woods or woodland edges), and has been replaced in cities by House Finches. Feeds primarily on seeds, with ash tree seeds a very important food source. Will visit seed feeders along with House Finches, making it hard to tell them apart. A rich loud song, with a distinctive "tic" note made only in flight. Not a purple color, the Latin species name *purpureus* means "crimson" or other reddish color.

female
pg. 335

male

SUMMER TANAGER
Piranga rubra

SUMMER

Size: 8" (20 cm)

Male: Bright rosy red bird with darker red wings.

Female: overall yellow with slightly darker wings

Juvenile: male has patches of red and green over the entire body, female is same as adult female

Nest: cup; female builds; 1-2 broods per year

Eggs: 3-5; pale blue with dark markings

Incubation: 10-12 days; female incubates

Fledging: unknown days; female and male feed young

Migration: complete, to Central and South America

Food: insects, fruit

Compare: Similar size as the male Northern Cardinal (pg. 293), but Cardinal has a black mask, large crest and red bill.

Stan's Notes: Found throughout Virginia where woodlands exist, especially in mixed pine and oak forest. Due to land clearing for agriculture, populations have decreased over the past century and especially during the last two decades. Returning to the state in late April and with young hatching in late May, some pairs have two broods per year. While fruit makes up some of the diet, most of it consists of insects such as bees and wasps. The Summer Tanager unfortunately seems to be parasitized by Brown-headed Cowbirds.

female pg. 139

male

NORTHERN CARDINAL
Cardinalis cardinalis

YEAR-ROUND

Size: 8-9" (20-22.5 cm)

Male: All-red bird with a black mask that extends from the face down to the chin and throat. Large red bill and crest.

Female: buff brown with tinges of red on crest and wings, same black mask and red bill

Juvenile: same as female, but with a blackish gray bill

Nest: cup; female builds; 2-3 broods per year

Eggs: 3-4; bluish white with brown markings

Incubation: 12-13 days; female and male incubate

Fledging: 9-10 days; female and male feed young

Migration: non-migrator

Food: seeds, insects, fruit; comes to seed feeders

Compare: Similar size as the male Summer Tanager (pg. 291), but the Tanager is rosy red. Look for Northern Cardinal's black mask, large crest and red bill.

Stan's Notes: A familiar backyard bird. Look for the male feeding female during courtship. Male feeds young of the first brood by himself while female builds second nest. The name comes from the Latin word *cardinalis*, which means "important." Very territorial in spring, it will fight its own reflection in a window. Non-territorial during winter, gathering in small flocks of up to 20 birds. Both the male and female sing, and can be heard anytime of year. Listen for its "whata-cheer-cheer-cheer" territorial call in spring.

in flight

LEAST TERN
Sterna antillarum

Size: 9" (22.5 cm)

Male: A white and gray tern with black cap, white forehead. Bill is light orange-yellow with a dark tip. White belly. Legs are same color as the bill. Black wing tips and a short, deeply forked tail, seen in flight.

Female: same as male

Juvenile: browner version of adult, has dark bill and partial black cap during first summer

Nest: ground; female builds; 1 brood per year

Eggs: 1-3; olive green with dark markings

Incubation: 20-22 days; female incubates

Fledging: 19-20 days; female teaches young to feed

Migration: complete, to South America

Food: aquatic insects, fish

Compare: Half the size of Royal Tern (pg. 303), which has black legs and a large orange-red bill, unlike Least's smaller, lighter orange-yellow bill with a dark tip. In flight, look for black wing tips and a short, deeply forked tail.

Stan's Notes: The smallest tern in North America, the Least Tern is also an endangered species in many North American locations. Killed by the hundreds of thousands in the early 1900s for its feathers, its decreasing numbers are now due to predators, such as cats and dogs, and human disturbance while nesting. Nests in large colonies on sandy beaches. Will often hover over intruders in the colony. Hunts small fish and aquatic insects by plunging into water or skimming over the surface. Recognizes mate by distinctive calls.

295

in flight

FORSTER'S TERN
Sterna forsteri

Size: 14-15" (36-38 cm)

Male: A white and gray tern with jet black crown and an orange bill with a black tip. Leading edge of wings is gray, trailing edge is white. Characteristic forked tail is long and white. Winter plumage lacks black crown and bill becomes nearly entirely black.

Female: same as male

Juvenile: similar to adult, lacks the black crown

Nest: platform; female and male build; 1 brood per year

Eggs: 3-5; tan to white with brown markings

Incubation: 23-24 days; female and male incubate

Fledging: 24-26 days; male and female feed young

Migration: complete, to southern coastal states, Mexico and Central America

Food: small fish, aquatic insects

Compare: Smaller than Royal Tern (pg. 303), which has larger orange-red bill. Look for jet black crown, orange bill with black tip and white tips of wings. The Least Tern (pg. 295) is smaller and has a lighter orange yellow bill.

Stan's Notes: Usually seen in small colonies. Catches small fish by diving into the water headfirst. Will catch insects in flight. Builds a platform nest on floating vegetation. Nests along coastal Virginia in shallow-water marshes. Named after Johann Reinhold Forster, a German naturalist who traveled around the world with Captain Cook in 1772.

winter

breeding

LAUGHING GULL
Larus atricilla

YEAR-ROUND
MIGRATION

Size: 16-17" (40-43 cm); up to 3⅓-foot wingspan

Male: Breeding adult has black head "hood," and white neck, chest and belly. Slate gray back and wings with black wing tips, and orange bill. Winter plumage lacks the "hood" and has a black bill.

Female: same as male

Juvenile: brown throughout, gray sides, lacking the black head and white chest, has a gray bill

Nest: ground; the male and female build; 1 brood per year

Eggs: 2-4; olive with brown markings

Incubation: 18-20 days; female and male incubate

Fledging: 30-35 days; male and female feed young

Migration: complete, to East and Gulf coasts, Mexico, Central and South America, non-migrator to partial migrator in Virginia

Food: fish, insects, aquatic insects

Compare: Smaller than the Ring-billed Gull (pg. 301) and Herring Gull (pg. 309). Look for black head "hood," and slate gray back and wings of Laughing Gull.

Stan's Notes: This is a three-year gull that starts out mostly brown and gray. The second year it resembles adults, but lacks a complete black head "hood." Breeding plumage in the third year. Male tosses its head back and calls to attract a mate. Nests in marshes in large colonies. Nest is a scrape on the ground lined with grass, sticks and rocks. Adults feed young a half-digested regurgitant.

winter

juvenile

breeding

RING-BILLED GULL
Larus delawarensis

WINTER

Size: 19" (48 cm); up to 4-foot wingspan

Male: A white bird with gray wings, black wing tips spotted with white, and a white tail, as seen in flight. Yellow bill with a black ring near tip. Yellowish legs and feet. Winter or non-breeding adult has a speckled brown back of head and nape of neck.

Female: same as male

Juvenile: mostly gray version of adult, has dark band at end of tail

Nest: ground; the female and male build; 1 brood per year

Eggs: 2-4; off-white with brown markings

Incubation: 20-21 days; female and male incubate

Fledging: 20-40 days; female and male feed young

Migration: complete, to Virginia and southern coastal states, Mexico

Food: insects, fish; scavenges for food

Compare: Similar to Herring Gull (pg. 309), which has an orange mark on tip of lower bill. Herring Gull has pink legs and feet, and lacks Ring-billed's black ring.

Stan's Notes: A common gull of garbage dumps and parking lots. Extremely common winter gull in Virginia, it's expanding its range and remaining farther north longer in the winter due to successful scavenging in cities. A three-year gull with a new, different plumage in each of the first three autumns. Attains ring on bill after its first winter. Doesn't attain adult plumage until the third year.

winter

in flight

breeding

ROYAL TERN
Sterna maxima

YEAR-ROUND
SUMMER

Size: 20" (50 cm)

Male: Gray back and upper surface of wings with white below. Large orange-red bill. Forked tail. Black legs and feet. Breeding plumage has a black cap extending down the nape. Winter plumage has a white forehead and only a partial black cap.

Female: same as male

Juvenile: dull white to gray with only a hint of black cap that rarely extends down nape

Nest: ground; female and male build; 1-2 broods per year

Eggs: 1-2; off-white with dark brown markings

Incubation: 30-31 days; female and male incubate

Fledging: 28-35 days; female and male feed young

Migration: complete, to coasts of Mexico, Central and South America, partial to non-migrator in coastal Virginia

Food: fish, aquatic insects

Compare: Larger than Forster's Tern (pg. 297), which has a small black-tipped bill. Twice the size of Least Tern (pg. 295), which has a lighter orange-yellow bill and a shorter forked tail.

Stan's Notes: A resident in coastal Virginia, rarely seen away from the coast. Nests in large colonies. Lays one egg (rarely two) in a shallow depression on the ground. Like other terns, the Royal Tern plunges from heights 40 feet (12 m) and more into water headfirst to capture fish and aquatic insects.

CATTLE EGRET
Bubulcus ibis

Size: 20" (50 cm)

Male: Stocky with a disproportional large round head. White with orange buff crest, breast and back. Red-orange bill and legs. Winter plumage is all white with a yellow bill and dark legs.

Female: same as male

Juvenile: similar to winter adult, with a dark bill

Nest: platform; female and male build; 1 brood per year

Eggs: 2-5; light blue green without markings

Incubation: 22-26 days; female and male incubate

Fledging: 28-30 days; female and male feed young

Migration: partial, to southern states, Mexico, Central and South America; moves to find food

Food: insects, small mammals

Compare: About half the size of Great Egret (pg. 315), which has a much longer neck and a much larger bill. White Ibis (pg. 311) has a long orange-to-red down-curved bill.

Stan's Notes: Came to South America from Africa around 1880, reaching Florida in the 1940s, spreading northward since its arrival. Frequently seen singularly in pastures, hunting insects at cow and horse pies. Holding its head still while wiggling its neck back and forth and from side to side, it stabs at prey, captures it, then tosses it to the back of its mouth in one swift move. It is often attracted to field fires to hunt newly exposed animals and insects. In some years it is found as far as northern tier states and Canada.

SNOWY EGRET
Egretta thula

Size: 24" (60 cm)

Male: All-white bird with black bill and legs, and bright yellow feet. Long feather plumes on the head, neck and back during breeding season.

Female: same as male

Juvenile: similar to adult, but backs of legs are yellow

Nest: platform; female and male build; 1 brood per year

Eggs: 3-5; light blue-green without markings

Incubation: 20-24 days; female and male incubate

Fledging: 28-30 days; female and male feed young

Migration: complete, to Gulf coast and Mexico, partial migrator in Virginia

Food: aquatic insects, fish

Compare: Much smaller than Great Egret (pg. 315), which has black feet and yellow bill. Same size as juvenile Little Blue Heron (pg. 87), which has a black-tipped gray bill.

Stan's Notes: Common in wetlands and often seen with other egrets, colonies may include up to several hundred nests. Nests are low in shrubs 5 to 10 feet (1.5 to 3 m) tall or are on the ground, usually mixed among other egret and heron nests. Chicks hatch days apart (asynchronous), leading to starvation of last to hatch. Will actively "hunt" prey by moving around quickly, stirring up small fish and aquatic insects with its feet. In the breeding state, a yellow patch at base of the bill and yellow feet turn orange-red. Was hunted to near extinction in the late 1800s for its feathers.

breeding

winter

HERRING GULL
Larus argentatus

Size: 23-26" (58-66 cm); up to 5-foot wingspan

Male: Snow-white bird with slate gray wings and black wing tips with tiny white spots. Bill is yellow with an orange-red spot near tip of the lower bill. Pinkish legs. Winter plumage head and neck are dirty gray to brown.

Female: same as male

Juvenile: uniformly mottled brown to gray, black bill

Nest: ground; the female and male build; 1 brood per year

Eggs: 2-3; olive with brown markings

Incubation: 24-28 days; female and male incubate

Fledging: 35-36 days; female and male feed young

Migration: complete, to coasts that remain unfrozen in North America; winters in Virginia

Food: fish, insects, clams, eggs, baby birds

Compare: Larger than the Ring-billed Gull (pg. 301), which has yellowish legs and a black ring around its bill, and lacks an orange-red dot on the lower mandible.

Stan's Notes: Common gull of large lakes. An opportunistic bird, scavenging for food from dumpsters, but will also take other birds' eggs and young right from nest. Often drops clams and other shellfish from heights to break shells and get to the soft interior. Nests in colonies, returning to same site year after year. Lines ground nest with grasses and seaweed. Takes about four years for juveniles to obtain adult plumage. Adults molt to a dirty gray in the winter, and look similar to juveniles.

309

juvenile

WHITE IBIS
Eudocimus albus

SUMMER

Size: 25" (63 cm); up to 3-foot wingspan

Male: All-white bird with a very long, downward-curved orange-to-red bill. Pink facial skin. Leg color matches the bill. Black wing tips, seen only in flight.

Female: same as male, but smaller and with less of a down-curved bill

Juvenile: combination of chocolate brown and white for the first two years, dull orange bill

Nest: platform; female and male build; 1 brood per year

Eggs: 2-3; light blue with dark markings

Incubation: 21-23 days; female and male incubate

Fledging: 28-35 days; female and male feed young

Migration: complete, to coastal Georgia and Florida

Food: aquatic insects, crustaceans, fish

Compare: One of two ibis species in Virginia, the long, down-curved bill helps identify them. The White Ibis is all white and not confused with the brown Glossy Ibis (pg. 197).

Stan's Notes: Increasing in Virginia over the past 50 years, with inland sightings becoming more common. Prefers fresh water over salt water, with crayfish a big part of the diet. White plumage with black wing tips and a bright orange-to-red down-curved bill make this bird easy to identify. Often seen flying in groups of 30 or more. Nests in large colonies in well-made stick nests.

blue morph

white morph

SNOW GOOSE
Chen caerulescens

MIGRATION
WINTER

Size: 25-38" (63-96 cm)

Male: A mostly white goose with varying patches of black and brown. Black wing tips. Pink bill and legs. Some birds are grayish with a white head.

Female: same as male

Juvenile: overall dull gray with a dark bill

Nest: ground; female builds; 1 brood per year

Eggs: 3-5; white without markings

Incubation: 23-25 days; female incubates

Fledging: 45-49 days; female and male teach young to feed

Migration: complete, to the East coast, southern states and Mexico

Food: aquatic insects and plants

Compare: Much smaller than Tundra Swan (pg. 317), lacking Tundra's black bill and legs. Smaller than the Canada Goose (pg. 269), lacking black neck and white chin strap.

Stan's Notes: Two color morphs. The more common white morph is pure white with black wing tips. Gray morph is often called blue, with a white head, gray chest and back, and pink bill and legs. Has a thick serrated bill for pulling up plants. Breeds in large colonies on the tundra of northern Canada. Females don't breed until they are 2 to 3 years old. Older females produce more eggs and are more successful than the younger females. Seen by the thousands during migration, arriving in November and leaving in March.

GREAT EGRET
Ardea alba

YEAR-ROUND
MIGRATION
SUMMER

Size: 38" (96 cm)

Male: Tall, thin, elegant all-white bird with long, pointed yellow bill. Black stilt-like legs and black feet.

Female: same as male

Juvenile: same as adult

Nest: platform; male and female build; 1 brood per year

Eggs: 2-3; light blue without markings

Incubation: 23-26 days; female and male incubate

Fledging: 43-49 days; female and male feed young

Migration: complete, to southern coastal states, partial migrator to non-migrator in coastal Virginia

Food: fish, aquatic insects, frogs, crayfish

Compare: The Snowy Egret (pg. 307) is much smaller with yellow feet and a black bill vs. Great Egret's black feet and yellow bill. Almost twice the size of the Cattle Egret (pg. 305), which has a much shorter neck and smaller bill. Larger than juvenile Little Blue Heron (pg. 87), which has a black-tipped gray bill.

Stan's Notes: A tall and stately bird, the Great Egret slowly stalks shallow wetlands looking for small fish to spear with its long sharp bill. Nests in colonies of up to 100 birds. Now protected, they were hunted to near extinction in the 1800s and early 1900s for their long white plumage. The name "Egret" came from the French word *aigrette*, which means "ornamental tufts of plumes." The plumes grow near the tail during breeding season.

in flight

TUNDRA SWAN
Cygnus columbianus

MIGRATION
WINTER

Size: 50-54" (127-137 cm); up to 5½-ft. wingspan

Male: Large all-white swan with all-black bill, legs and feet. Has a small yellow mark in front of eyes.

Female: same as male

Juvenile: same size as adult, gray plumage, pinkish gray bill

Nest: ground; the female and male build; 1 brood per year

Eggs: 4-5; creamy white without markings

Incubation: 35-40 days; female and male incubate

Fledging: 60-70 days; female and male feed young

Migration: complete, to the East coast

Food: plants, aquatic insects

Compare: Snow Goose (pg. 313) is much smaller and has black wing tips. Look for the black bill and legs.

Stan's Notes: Nests on the tundra of northern Canada and Alaska, hence its common name. Migrates diagonally across North America to reach wintering grounds along the East coast. Gathers in large numbers in some lakes and rivers to rest, usually staying until the water freezes before continuing to migrate. Flies in large V-shaped wedges. Often seen in large family groups consisting of 20 or more individuals. The young are easy to distinguish by their overall gray color and pinkish bill. Gives a high-pitched, whistle-like call.

male

winter male

female

AMERICAN GOLDFINCH
Carduelis tristis

YEAR-ROUND

Size: 5" (13 cm)

Male: A perky yellow bird with a black patch on forehead. Black tail with conspicuous white rump. Black wings with white wing bars. No marking on the chest. Dramatic change in color during winter, similar to female.

Female: dull olive yellow without a black forehead, with brown black wings and white rump

Juvenile: same as female

Nest: cup; female builds; 1 brood per year

Eggs: 4-6; pale blue without markings

Incubation: 10-12 days; female incubates

Fledging: 11-17 days; female and male feed young

Migration: partial migrator to non-migrator; flocks of up to 20 move around North America

Food: seeds, insects; will come to seed feeders

Compare: Male Yellow Warbler (pg. 323) is all yellow with orange streaking on chest. Pine Siskin (pg. 95) has a streaked chest and belly, with yellow wing bars. The female House Finch (pg. 97) and female Purple Finch (pg. 111) both have heavily streaked chests.

Stan's Notes: Year-round resident most often found in open fields, scrubby areas and woodlands. Often called Wild Canary. A feeder bird that enjoys Nyger Thistle. Late summer nesting, uses the silky down from wild thistle for nest. Appears roller-coaster-like during flight. Listen for it to twitter in flight. Almost always in small flocks. In northern states, moves only far enough south to find food.

319

COMMON YELLOWTHROAT
Geothlypis trichas

YEAR-ROUND
SUMMER

Size: 5" (13 cm)

Male: Olive brown bird with bright yellow throat and breast, a white belly and a distinctive black mask outlined in white. A long, thin, pointed black bill.

Female: same as male, but lacking the black mask

Juvenile: same as female

Nest: cup; female builds; 2 broods per year

Eggs: 3-5; white with brown markings

Incubation: 11-12 days; female incubates

Fledging: 10-11 days; female and male feed young

Migration: complete, southern states, Mexico, Central America, non-migrator in eastern Virginia

Food: insects

Compare: Found in a similar habitat as the American Goldfinch (pg. 319), but lacks the male's black forehead and wings. The male Yellow Warbler (pg. 323) has fine orange streaks on chest and lacks the black mask. Yellow-rumped Warbler (pg. 221) has only spots of yellow, compared with the Yellowthroat's yellow breast.

Stan's Notes: A common warbler of open fields and marshes. Has a cheerful, well-known song, "witchity-witchity-witchity-witchity." The male performs a curious courtship display, bouncing in and out of tall grass while uttering an unusual song. The young remain dependent upon the parents longer than most warblers. A frequent cowbird host.

male

female

YELLOW WARBLER
Dendroica petechia

Size: 5" (13 cm)

Male: Yellow warbler with orange streaks on the chest and belly. Long, pointed dark bill.

Female: same as male, but lacking orange streaking

Juvenile: similar to female, only much duller

Nest: cup; female builds; 1 brood per year

Eggs: 4-5; white with brown markings

Incubation: 11-12 days; female incubates

Fledging: 10-12 days; female and male feed young

Migration: complete, to southern states, Mexico, and Central and South America

Food: insects

Compare: Yellow-rumped Warbler (pg. 221) has only spots of yellow, compared with the orange streaking on chest of male Yellow Warbler. Male American Goldfinch (pg. 319) has black wings and forehead. Female Warbler is similar to the female American Goldfinch (pg. 319), but lacks the white wing bars.

Stan's Notes: A scattered but widespread warbler in Virginia. Seen in gardens and shrubby areas close to water. A prolific insect eater, gleaning small caterpillars and other insects from tree leaves. The male is often seen higher up in trees than the female. Female is less conspicuous. Seen during migration, starting in August. Returns in April. The males arrive a week or two before the females to claim territories. Migrates at night in mixed flocks of warblers. Rests and feeds days.

SUMMER

PRAIRIE WARBLER
Dendroica discolor

Size: 5" (13 cm)

Male: Olive back with chestnut-colored streaks. Bright yellow from the chin to belly. Black streaks on sides from neck down. Black line through eyes. Yellow eyebrows.

Female: same as male, only duller

Juvenile: similar to female

Nest: cup; female builds; 2 broods per year

Eggs: 3-5; white with brown markings

Incubation: 11-14 days; female incubates

Fledging: 8-11 days; female and male feed young

Migration: complete, to the Caribbean

Food: insects

Compare: The Yellow Warbler (pg. 323) lacks black streaks and a black line through the eyes. Prairie Warbler lacks the complete black mask of Common Yellowthroat (pg. 321). Watch for Prairie Warbler to twitch its tail when feeding.

Stan's Notes: A common and widespread warbler in the state. Returns to Virginia in mixed flocks of warblers in late April to mid-May. It was unfortunately misnamed "Prairie" when first found in a barren area in Kentucky. Nests in dry, brushy clearings and forest edges, making it a perfect host for Brown-headed Cowbirds. Will sometimes desert a parasitized nest. Nests in upright fork of a tree. Feeds young mainly caterpillars.

PALM WARBLER
Dendroica palmarum

MIGRATION
WINTER

Size: 5½" (14 cm)

Male: Distinctive yellow eyebrows. Yellow throat, belly and undertail. An obvious chestnut-colored crown. On the sides of breast, thin chestnut-colored streaks. A dark line across dark eyes.

Female: same as male

Juvenile: same as adult, but duller and brown

Nest: cup; female builds; 1-2 broods per year

Eggs: 4-5; white with brown markings

Incubation: 11-12 days; female incubates

Fledging: 12-13 days; female and male feed young

Migration: complete, to southeastern coastal states, the West Indies and Central America

Food: insects, fruit

Compare: Similar size as the Yellow-rumped Warbler (pg. 221), but Yellow-rumped lacks yellow throat and belly. Pine Warbler (pg. 329) has pronounced white wing bars. Look for the yellow eyebrows and chestnut cap.

Stan's Notes: Most common during migration and becoming less common in the winter. Frequently seen in woodland during migration. Look for it to wag or bob its tail while gleaning insects from leaves and flowers of trees. One of the few warblers to feed on the ground. Hops rather than walks. Nests at the edge of northern spruce bogs. Recognizes and destroys cowbird eggs, burying them with its nest, which it builds over the top of the cowbird nest.

PINE WARBLER
Dendroica pinus

YEAR-ROUND
SUMMER

Size: 5½" (14 cm)

Male: A yellow throat and breast with faint black streaks on sides of breast. Olive green back. Two white wing bars. White belly.

Female: similar to male, only paler

Juvenile: similar to adults, only browner, more white on belly

Nest: cup; female builds; 2-3 broods per year

Eggs: 3-5; white with brown markings

Incubation: 10-12 days; female incubates

Fledging: 12-14 days; female and male feed young

Migration: complete, to southern states, non-migrator in southeastern Virginia

Food: insects, seeds, fruit

Compare: Similar to Palm Warbler (pg. 327), lacking the brown cap and yellow eyebrows of the Palm. The Pine Warbler has much more pronounced white wing bars than the Palm.

Stan's Notes: A common resident of pine forest in Virginia. Builds nest only in pine forest. Brighter in spring and more drab in fall, it varies in color depending upon the time of year. Thought to have a larger bill than other warblers. Sometimes easier to identify by song than sight. Listen for a twittering, musical song that varies in speed. While most warblers are migrators, this species is non-migratory in southeastern Virginia. Populations increase in fall and winter with the arrival of northern birds.

male pg. 283

female

BALTIMORE ORIOLE
Icterus galbula

MIGRATION
SUMMER

Size: 7-8" (18-20 cm)

Female: A pale yellow bird with orange tones, gray brown wings, white wing bars, a gray bill and dark eyes.

Male: bright flaming orange bird with black head and black extending down nape of neck onto the back, black wings with white and orange wing bars, an orange tail with black streaks, gray bill and dark eyes

Juvenile: same as female

Nest: pendulous; female builds; 1 brood per year

Eggs: 4-5; bluish with brown markings

Incubation: 12-14 days; female incubates

Fledging: 12-14 days; female and male feed young

Migration: complete, to Mexico, Central America and South America

Food: insects, fruit, nectar; comes to orange half and nectar feeders

Compare: Very similar to the female Orchard Oriole (pg. 333), which lacks orange tones and has less pronounced wing bars.

Stan's Notes: A fantastic songster, often heard before seen. Easily attracted to a feeder offering grape jelly, orange halves or sugar water (nectar). Parents bring young to feeders. Sits in tops of trees feeding on caterpillars. Female builds a sock-like nest at outermost branches of tall trees. Often returns to the same area year after year. Some of the last birds to arrive in spring (March to April) and first to leave in fall (August). Breeds throughout Virginia.

male pg. 285

female

ORCHARD ORIOLE
Icterus spurius

SUMMER

Size: 7-8" (18-20 cm)

Female: An olive green bird with a dull yellow belly. Two white wing bars on dark gray wings. Long, thin black bill with a small gray mark on lower mandible (jaw).

Male: dull orange with a black head, chin, upper back, wings and tail, single white wing bars

Juvenile: same as female, black bib on first-year male

Nest: pendulous; female builds; 1 brood per year

Eggs: 3-5; pale blue to white, brown markings

Incubation: 11-12 days; female and male incubate

Fledging: 11-14 days; female and male feed young

Migration: complete, central Mexico, Central America and northern South America

Food: insects, fruit; comes to fruit/nectar feeders

Compare: Similar to female Baltimore Oriole (pg. 331), which has orange overtones and more pronounced wing bars. The female Summer Tanager (pg. 335) is mustard yellow with a larger, thicker bill.

Stan's Notes: Prefers orchards or open woods, hence its common name. Eats insects until wild fruit starts to ripen. One of the last birds to arrive in spring and one of the first to leave in fall. Spends only four to five months in Virginia. Often migrates with the more abundant Baltimore Oriole. Usually nests alone; sometimes nests in small colonies. Parents bring young to jelly and orange half feeders just after fledging. Many think the orioles have left in summer, but the birds are concentrating on finding insects to feed their young.

male pg. 291

female

SUMMER TANAGER
Piranga rubra

SUMMER

Size: 8" (20 cm)

Female: Some show a faint wash of red, but most females are a mustard yellow overall with slightly darker wings.

Male: bright rosy red bird with darker red wings

Juvenile: male has patches of red and green over the entire body, female is same as adult female

Nest: cup; female builds; 1-2 broods per year

Eggs: 3-5; pale blue with dark markings

Incubation: 10-12 days; female incubates

Fledging: unknown days; female and male feed young

Migration: complete, to Central and South America

Food: insects, fruit

Compare: Similar to female Orchard Oriole (pg. 333) and Baltimore Oriole (pg. 331). The female Summer Tanager lacks wing bars and has a larger bill.

Stan's Notes: Found throughout Virginia where woodlands exist, especially in mixed pine and oak forest. Due to land clearing for agriculture, populations have decreased over the past century and especially during the last two decades. Returning to the state in late April and with young hatching in late May, some pairs have two broods per year. While fruit makes up some of the diet, most of it consists of insects such as bees and wasps. The Summer Tanager unfortunately seems to be parasitized by Brown-headed Cowbirds.

EASTERN MEADOWLARK
Sturnella magna

YEAR-ROUND

Size: 9" (22.5 cm)

Male: Robin-shaped bird with brown back, yellow chest and belly, and a prominent black V-shaped necklace. White outer tail feathers.

Female: same as male

Juvenile: same as adult

Nest: cup, on the ground in dense cover; female builds; 2 broods per year

Eggs: 3-5; white with brown markings

Incubation: 13-15 days; female incubates

Fledging: 11-12 days; female and male feed young

Migration: complete, to southern states, Mexico and Central America, non-migrator in Virginia

Food: insects, seeds

Compare: The only large yellow bird with a black V mark on chest.

Stan's Notes: A bird of open grassy country. Named "Meadowlark" because it's a bird of meadows and sings like the larks of Europe. Best known for its wonderful song–a flute-like, clear whistle. Often seen perching on fence posts, it will quickly dive into tall grass if approached. Conspicuous white markings on each side of its tail, most often seen when flying away. Nest is sometimes domed with dried grass. Not a member of the lark family, it actually belongs to the blackbird family. Related to grackles and orioles.

HELPFUL RESOURCES:

Birder's Bug Book, The. Waldbauer, Gilbert. Cambridge: Harvard University Press, 1998.

Birder's Dictionary. Cox, Randall T. Helena, MT: Falcon Press Publishing, 1996.

Birder's Handbook, The. Ehrlich, Paul R., David S. Dobkin and Darryl Wheye. New York: Simon and Schuster, 1988.

Birds Do It, Too: The Amazing Sex Life of Birds. Harrison, Kit and George H. Harrison. Minocqua, WI: Willow Creek Press, 1997.

Birds of Forest, Yard, and Thicket. Eastman, John. Mechanicsburg, PA: Stackpole Books, 1997.

Birds of North America. Kaufman, Kenn. New York: Houghton Mifflin, 2000.

Blackbirds of the Americas. Orians, Gordon H. Seattle: University of Washington Press, 1985.

Cardinal, The. Osborne, June. Austin: University of Texas Press, 1995.

Dictionary of American Bird Names, The. Choate, Ernest A. Boston: Harvard Common Press, 1985.

Everything You Never Learned About Birds. Rupp, Rebecca. Pownal, VT: Storey Publishing, 1997.

Field Guide to the Birds, A: A Completely New Guide to All the Birds of Eastern and Central North America. Peterson, Roger Tory and Virginia Marie Peterson. Boston: Houghton Mifflin, 1998.

Field Guide to the Birds of North America: Third Edition. Washington, DC: National Geographic Society, 1999.

Field Guide to Warblers of North America, A. Dunn, Jon and Kimball Garrett. Boston: Houghton Mifflin, 1997.

Folklore of Birds. Martin, Laura C. Old Saybrook, CT: Globe Pequot Press, 1996.

Guide to Bird Behavior, A: Vol I, II, III. Stokes, Donald and Lillian Stokes. Boston: Little, Brown and Company, 1989.

How Birds Migrate. Kerlinger, Paul. Mechanicsburg, PA: Stackpole Books, 1995

Lives of Birds, The: Birds of the World and Their Behavior. Short, Lester L. Collingdale, PA: DIANE Publishing, 2000.

Lives of North American Birds. Kaufman, Kenn. Boston: Houghton Mifflin, 1996.

Living on the Wind. Weidensaul, Scott. New York: North Point Press, 2000.

National Audubon Society: North American Birdfeeder Handbook. Burton, Robert. New York: Dorling Kindersley Publishing, 1995.

National Audubon Society: The Sibley Guide to Bird Life and Behavior. Edited by David Allen Sibley, Chris Elphick and John B. Dunning, Jr. New York: Alfred A. Knopf, 2001.

National Audubon Society: The Sibley Guide to Birds. Sibley, David Allen. New York: Alfred A. Knopf, 2000.

Photographic Guide to North American Raptors, A. Wheeler, Brian K. and William S. Clark. New York: Academic Press, 1999.

Secret Lives of Birds, The. Gingras, Pierre. Toronto: Key Porter Books, 1997.

Secrets of the Nest. Dunning, Joan. Boston: Houghton Mifflin, 1994.

Sparrows and Buntings: A Guide to the Sparrows and Buntings of North America and the World. Byers, Clive, Jon Curson and Urban Olsson. New York: Houghton Mifflin, 1995.

Stokes Bluebird Book: The Complete Guide to Attracting Bluebirds. Stokes, Donald and Lillian Stokes. Boston: Little, Brown and Company, 1991.

Stokes Field Guide to Birds: Eastern Region. Stokes, Donald and Lillian Stokes. Boston: Little, Brown and Company, 1996.

Stokes Purple Martin Book. Stokes, Donald and Lillian Stokes. Boston: Little, Brown and Company, 1997.

For reporting unusual bird sightings or to hear a recording of where birds have been seen, contact:

The Virginia Birdline
757-238-2713

WEB PAGES:

The Internet is a valuable place to learn about birds. Following are web sites to assist you in your pursuit of birds. You may find birding on the net a fun way to learn more about birds or spend a long winter night.

SITE	ADDRESS
The Virginia Society of Ornithology	www.ecoventures-travel.com/vso
American Birding Association	www.americanbirding.org
Cornell Lab of Ornithology	www.birds.cornell.edu
Author Stan Tekiela's home page	www.naturesmart.com

Use the boxes to check the birds you've seen.

ABOUT THE AUTHOR:

Stan Tekiela is a naturalist, author and wildlife photographer with a Bachelor of Science degree in Natural History from the University of Minnesota. He has been a professional naturalist for over 20 years and is a member of the Minnesota Naturalist Association, the Outdoor Writers Association of America and Canon Professional Services. Stan actively studies and photographs birds throughout the U.S. He received an Excellence in Interpretation award from the National Association for Interpretation, and a regional award for Commitment to Outdoor Education. A columnist and radio personality, his syndicated column appears in more than 20 cities and he can be heard on a number of radio stations. Stan resides in Victoria, Minnesota, with wife Katherine and daughter Abigail. He can be contacted via his web page at www.naturesmart.com.

OTHER BOOKS BY STAN TEKIELA:

Birds of the Carolinas Field Guide
Birds of Georgia Field Guide
Birds of Kentucky Field Guide
Trees of Minnesota Field Guide
Wildflowers of Ohio Field Guide
Nature Smart: A Family Guide to Nature
Start Mushrooming: The Easiest Way to Collect Edible Mushrooms